THE
CLONE

THE
CLONE

HERALDING THE COMING OF JESUS

CRAIG H. SWAIN

CITI OF
BOOKS

CITIOFBOOKS, INC.
3736 Eubank NE Suite A1
Albuquerque, NM 87111-3579
www.citiofbooks.com
Hotline: 1 (877) 389-2759
Fax: 1 (505) 930-7244

Ordering Information:
Quantity sales. Special discounts are available on quantity purchases by corporations, associations, and others. For details, contact the publisher at the address above.

Printed in the United States of America.

ISBN-13:	Softcover	978-1-962366-70-0
	eBook	978-1-962366-71-7

Library of Congress Control Number: 2023920175

1. INT. THE SHROUD OF TURIN—ESTABLISHING 1

We see the Shroud of Turin as it is in all its ghostly magnificence. The Introduction crawls over the Shroud and slowly zooms into the top of the fabric. We hear the song "What If God Was One of Us" by Joan Osborne play as the introduction rolls over the face of the shroud.

INTRODUCTION

The Shroud of Turin is believed by many millions to be one of two burial cloths of Jesus Christ, the Jewish Messiah, from the tomb of Joseph of Arimathea. It has been on public display intermittently since the thirteenth century. Many billions more, however, do not believe.

Customarily, the deceased was laid on a shroud, which was then folded over the body. Shrouds are approximately fourteen feet long.

The image on the shroud looks as if it was made by an intense light striking the cloth that acted as if it were photosensitive. Like putting an object on photosensitive paper and exposing it to light, the developed result would be a negative image: where the object blocked the light, the paper would be white; where there was no image, it would be black. This negative image on the shroud prevented any other perception than that of a series of irregular blotches.

The shroud was photographed in 1898 for the first time, and the image was reversed. The camera's film reversed the shroud's negative image, making it a positive image. The photographic process showed a man's face and body arising from the shroud.

2. INT. SAME SHOT OF SHROUD 2

We hear a camera shutter click. The shroud's image dissolves into a positive image that reveals the face. The introduction continues to crawl over the image.

INTRODUCTION

Scientists in the twentieth century have determined that the bloodstains on the shroud are type AB.

Type AB blood was on the small head cloth also allegedly found by the apostle John in the tomb of Jesus Christ. The Roman Catholic Church has kept the head cloth in safekeeping since the ninth century.

Many people question the fact that the shroud is two thou sand years old and that the image is of Jesus Christ.

The shroud is the most tested and studied relic in the history of mankind.

DISSOLVE TO:

3. INT. MONASTERY CORRIDOR—NIGHT 3

SUPER—3:00 AM, December, ten days before Christmas, Turin, Italy, 1992.

A dim corridor lined with doors ends at a dark-stained glass window that depicts Christ on the cross. Orange light flickers through the image, breathing life into the stained glass image.
Smoke rolls across the ceiling. A fire alarm shatters the silence. Emergency lights flash on and off.

Corridor doors fly open, and disheveled monks shuffle out and start to run down the corridor away from the stained glass window. We see the name on one door is Brother Jude Sindone. The door opens. Brother Jude peers out. In contrast to the other monks, he wears the brown cassock of his order. Brother Jude steps into the din, and Monk #1 runs into him, knocking them both off-balance.

MONK #1
Fire! Brother Jude, get out! Now!

Brother Jude calmly steps into the corridor and closes his door. He moves in the opposite direction of the other monks and toward the stained glass window above the doorway leading to the chapel. He walks toward the fire-opening doors of other rooms, apparently making sure no one is left behind. He looks back and sees that the corridor is empty. He is alone. He pulls his hood over his head, revealing that one hand is sheathed in a tight latex glove. He picks up his pace and disappears into the thickening smoke. He reaches the open doorway into the chapel and just inside, and to the right, he reaches for a crucifix hanging on the wall. The crucifix is upside down now. Brother Jude hesitates, looking perplexed. He grabs it fast and heads quickly towards the display casket containing the shroud.

4. INT. SHROUD OF TURIN DISPLAY CHAPEL— 'Continuing 4

The fire alarm continues to clang, but it is not as intense, muffled by distance. We see the display case where the Shroud of Turin lies in state. Hooded Brother Jude comes into view. His hands and face are hidden in his robes folds and hood, but when he gets to the casket, his gloved hand holding the crucifix materializes and strikes the shroud's protective glass shield. It breaks into jagged pieces. He reaches into the casket. With a pair of plastic surgical tweezers, he plucks bloodstained cloth strands from the shroud and puts them into a plastic bag.

Brother Jude starts to cough.

Someone else coughs. Brother Jude stops in his tracks. Emerging from the smoke is a very old long-bearded monk,

Brother Adrian, a Dustin Hoffman type, moves with painful difficulty.

BROTHER ADRIAN
What do you think you are doing?

Brother Jude puts the tweezers into the bag, seals it, and hides it in the folds of his robe. He turns to Brother Adrian, who arrives next to him.

BROTHER JUDE
Brother Adrian, help me get the shroud to safety!

Brother Jude moves to one end of the shroud case and reaches in. He picks an end of the shroud and starts to fold it up. Brother Adrian tries to catch up to him.

BROTHER ADRIAN
What were you doing? I saw you—

BROTHER JUDE
Saving the shroud! Hurry! Help me!

BROTHER ADRIAN

No! You were not! I saw you take something.
Let me see. Brother Adrian reaches for Brother Jude's robe.
He sees Brother Jude wearing a surgical glove on one hand.

BROTHER ADRIAN (continuing)

Why are you wearing that glove?

Brother Jude blocks Brother Adrian's reach and shoves him.
Brother Adrian loses his balance and falls backward into the shroud's case.
He hits his head and slips unconscious to the floor.

BROTHER JUDE

Oh God, no!

Brother Jude rushes to him as blood gushes onto the chapel floor.
He lifts Brother Adrian's head. He looks at his latex hand.
His hand is dripping blood.

BROTHER JUDE (continuing)

Damn!

Fire and smoke engulf the entire chapel. Brother Jude wipes this bloody glove on his robe. He pulls off the glove, tossing it towards the encroaching flames. He finishes folding the shroud.

Brother Jude is coughing constantly, and his breathing is labored and painful. He tries to lift Brother Adrian. He cannot, and he falls to the floor. He gets up. Brother Jude grabs Brother Adrian's arm and drags him away. He falls again. He reaches Brother Adrian alone but falls again. He sees the chapel doors. He cannot breathe. His tearing eyes lose focus, and he loses consciousness. In his other arm, he cradles the folded shroud to his chest.

The doors crash open, and firefighters enter.

5. INT. AMBULANCE—CONTINUING 5

Brother Jude lies on a gurney as the ambulance siren wails through the streets. An oxygen mask hides part of his face, which is streaked with soot and striped with tears. A paramedic wearing surgical gloves opens Brother

Jude's robe and begins to push on Brother Jude's chest. The cellophane bag slips partially out from its hiding place in his robe. Brother Jude moans. His eyelids flutter. He starts to cough.

> BROTHER JUDE
> Brother Adrian, Brother Adrian—my brother...

His voice is strained, punctuated with coughs.

> PARAMEDIC #1
> Lie still, brother. You are going to be all right.
> You are Brother Sindone, right?

> BROTHER JUDE
> Yes, yes, but where is Brother Adri—

> PARAMEDIC #1 (interrupting)
> You saved his life, brother.
> You're a hero! Now take it easy.

> BROTHER JUDE
> Brother Adrian...is alive! It is all my fault—

> PARAMEDIC #1
> Your brother is in a coma, but he is alive—thanks to you.
> Just relax now, it is going to be all right.

> BROTHER JUDE
> A coma! I am so sorry...

Brother Jude sees his cellophane bag sticking out. When Paramedic #1 looks away, he tucks it back into its hiding place and closes his eyes. He coughs.

6. INT. HOSPITAL ROOM—DAY 6

Brother Jude is sleeping in a private hospital room. A large crucifix hangs on the wall above and behind the bed. His eyes open slowly, and he sits up abruptly.

He reaches and grabs the headboard. He begins to pull himself up, out of the bed. Excruciating pain shoots through his body. He starts to cough and cry out and then starts to fall backward, grabbing the bedpost on the opposite side with his other hand. The camera pulls back to reveal the crucifix above the bed. Brother Jude is spread out much like Christ on the cross.

As his pain subsides, he can pull himself out of bed and shuffle over to the closet. He opens the doors and sighs in relief because he sees his smoky robe hanging there. With effort, he quickly reaches into the pocket to verify that the cellophane bag is still there. It is. He reaches back into the robe and pulls out a pre-addressed stamped envelope.

The camera does not stay on the envelope to see who it is addressed to. He opens the cellophane bag, takes the tweezers out, and throws them into the dark recesses of the closet corner. He closes the doors.

Brother Jude shuffles back to his bed. He sits and puts the cellophane bag into the envelope and seals it. We see that it is marked "Personal" and addressed to Mr. Clay Adams, International Cloning Institute, Edinburgh, Scotland. Brother Jude opens the drawer of the bedside dresser and puts the envelope in.

Brother Jude lies back on the bed. As his head hits the pil low, a door opens with a loud noise, but Brother Jude does not react as we hear the voice of Brother Superior.

BROTHER SUPERIOR
The hero lives! But can he talk?

Brother Jude struggles up as if by a reflex reaction to the authoritarian voice. He cannot get up. He coughs and lets his head fall back to the pillow.

BROTHER JUDE
Brother Superior, how is Brother Adrian?

BROTHER SUPERIOR
I'm afraid he is still in a coma. It is up to the Lord now.
We must put our faith in Him...
and you must rest and be healed yourself.

BROTHER JUDE

Yes, you are right, Brother Superior. I know, but I feel—

BROTHER SUPERIOR (interrupting)

You are not responsible for Brother Adrian's condition—
had you not been there to save the shroud, you would not have saved
Brother Adrian from the fire, and he would have perished.
You could have made it out on your own,
but you chose to help a brother who would not have been
able to save himself. (more)

BROTHER SUPERIOR (continued)

He hit his head quite hard when he was overcome by the smoke...
Thank the Lord the firefighters arrived in so timely a fashion.

BROTHER JUDE

Yes, I suppose you are right.

BROTHER SUPERIOR

Of course, I am right. You did what you could,
which was quite brave of you. Now what is it I can do for you?

BROTHER JUDE

Brother Superior, please open the drawer.
You'll see there is an envelope addressed to my brother in Scotland.

Brother Superior finds the envelope in the hospital dresser. As he
takes it from the drawer, we see that it is addressed care to the International
Cloning Institute to Clay Adams. It is marked "Personal."

BROTHER SUPERIOR

Consider it done, brother—it will be in this afternoon's post—however,
you should not expend your energy on letter writing...
you are here to rest and recover.

Brother Superior places the envelope in his robe and pats it with his
hand.

BROTHER SUPERIOR (continuing)
That reminds me, brother—I have good news for you.
Your old friend, Cardinal DeVille, has finally gotten
the approval for you to relocate to Rosslyn Monastery
so you will be near your brother—maybe if you take care of
yourself you'll be able to spend Christmas with us
at the monastery and get ready to relocate.

BROTHER JUDE
That is very good news. It is going to help my recovery greatly.

BROTHER SUPERIOR
I think that may be bad news for us, but we are happy that
it will be good for you. I have more news for you—are you ready for it?
Brother Superior looks directly into Brother Jude's eyes with the
seriousness of his office.

BROTHER SUPERIOR (continuing)
You have been granted an audience.

BROTHER JUDE
The Pope?

Brother Jude starts to frown at the thought of the Pope as if to ask why
the Pope would be interested in him.

BROTHER SUPERIOR
Yes, the Pope, silly, who else!

Brother Jude changes his perplexed look to a nod of acquiescence.

BROTHER SUPERIOR (continuing)
I wish you could take me with you Brother Jude—a private
audience is quite unusual you know.

BROTHER JUDE
You know the drill better than I do.

BROTHER SUPERIOR

No date has been set—your audience is contingent upon your good
health, brother. Think no more about it now...oh,
I probably have overstayed and tired you with all this on my first visit.
I should leave you now—I'll be back in a few days.

BROTHER JUDE

Thank you for taking the time to visit—you leave me with much to reflect
upon.
Brother Superior is moving towards the door to exit.

BROTHER JUDE (continuing)

Oh, brother—please pray for me.

BROTHER SUPERIOR

Of course, brother, we will all be praying for
you—you rest—that's an order.

7. EXT SAINT PETER'S SQUARE—DAY 7

SUPER—February 4, 1993

A crowd packs the square from corner to corner as the Pope walks
into view on the balcony. The Pope addresses the multitude in Italian as the
camera moves behind him.

8. INT. INNER SANCTUM—CONTINUING 8

The camera continues to move back to the vantage point of someone
behind him in the inner sanctum. We see Brother Jude standing next to
Cardinal DeVille, dressed in his formal red vestments. Other officials are
standing in the inner sanctum, listening to every word of the Pope.

CARDINAL DEVILLE

I shouldn't think he should be too much longer, Bill.

Brother Jude nods in agreement. The Pope's white vestments shimmer
in Rome's strong sun. The Pope raises his hand. Sunrays glint off his large
ring.

9. EXT. SAINT PETER'S SQUARE—CONTINUING 9

The Pope slowly drops his outstretched arm.

THE POPE (in Italian with subtitles)
Finally, concerning the Shroud of Turin—
the Holy Mother Church has never made a statement about to the
authenticity of the shroud. It is, therefore, still a personal
choice to believe or not believe according to each heart's desire.
Only until there is an official pronouncement will it become a matter of
faith and morals, after which every good Catholic will
have no more personal choice in the matter.
Thanks to Brother Jude Sindone, the shroud has once again
survived the flames of hell. May God bless each one of you.
The Pope blesses the multitude from left to right.

THE POPE (continuing)
In nomine patre etfilio et spiritu sancto.

10. INT. INNER SANCTUM—CONTINUING 10

The Pope finishes his benediction and exits the sun into the inner
sanctum. Everyone kneels. The Pope takes his first step into the Inner
Sanctum. A gust of wind blows his miter off his head. The miter falls in
front of an accolade, who picks it up. Two cardinals hastily grab it from him
and replace it with the Pope.

CARDINAL ONE (bowing)
Eminence.

The Pope passes Cardinal DeVille and Brother Jude as he walks to
large wooden doors that are opened by his attendants. They begin to stand
up. Brother Jude winces in pain and feebly gets to his feet. Cardinal DeVille
takes Brother Jude's arm to help him up and points him in the direction of
another exit.

CARDINAL DEVILLE
This way—we don't want to be late and miss this opportunity.

11. INT. VATICAN CORRIDOR—LATER

Ubiquitous religious art lines the dim corridor. It is barely seen in the dark surroundings. Cardinal DeVille is holding Brother Jude by the arm. Brother Jude wipes his sweating fore head with his free hand.

CARDINAL DEVILLE
Are you okay, Bill?

BROTHER JUDE
Yes, Jack—I just feel more like a groupie at a rock concert than—

CARDINAL DEVILLE (frowning)
Please control your tongue—you never know who is around here.

A large wooden door unlocks with the heavy noise of a medieval latch. Light floods through the corridor. The Pope appears, wearing his daily vestments and flanked by the two cardinals, who serve as orderlies. Cardinal DeVille steps forward, leaving Brother Jude behind as he approaches the Pope.

THE POPE
Cardinal DeVille—it is always so good to see you.

CARDINAL DEVILLE (bowing)
Your Holiness—may I introduce Brother Jude Sindone...
Brother Jude Steps forward, bowing. He coughs.

CARDINAL DEVILLE (continuing)
Brother Jude is here by your special invitation.

THE POPE
Warmest greetings, brother.

The Pope offers his ring. Brother Jude falls to his knees and kisses the Pope's ring.

BROTHER JUDE

Your Holiness, this is truly an honor, for I have long sought
to meet you personally.

Cardinal DeVille helps Brother Jude back on his feet.

THE POPE

We are informed that today is your birthday—thirty-three, is it?

BROTHER JUDE

Yes, Your Excellency. Thank you so much.

THE POPE

Ahh, to be thirty-three—that fateful age...

The Pope's orderlies make way for Brother Jude to walk with the Pope. They turn a corner into another dark corridor.

Brother Jude is having trouble keeping up with the Pope, even though the Pope's gait is slow and stately.

THE POPE (continuing)

We have been informed that you have taken an unusual
interest in the Shroud of Turin.

BROTHER JUDE

Oh yes, Excellency, I have been studying the—

THE POPE (interrupting)

You know, my son, you must not let your interests become
your obsession. Beware the past mistakes of the good brothers of the
Knights Templar. It will serve you well to remember
that fanaticism may lead to error.

BROTHER JUDE

I never considered myself in that light, Your Holiness... I... I just want to know the truth, and I want to share these truths with my brethren.

THE POPE

The truth! Yes, it would be helpful to know the truth if you look in the right place for it. Remember Pontius Pilate asked our Savior what is truth, and our Lord gave him no answer.

BROTHER JUDE

Yes, Holiness, I know the passage. Scripture also says, "Thy Word is truth."

THE POPE

That is the point. Only the Word of God is the truth, my son. Everything else may be a truth.. or a lie, as the case may be. In point of fact, the only time any human being may be speaking the Truth with a capital T is when he or she is quoting Scripture.

Brother Jude opens his mouth as if to speak. He stops him self. The realization of his station bears down on his shoulders, and he slumps in submission.

THE POPE (continuing)

We think it best that you put no more in writing about the shroud at this time...we understand that you have been approved to relocate to Scotland at your convenience. Perhaps Cardinal DeVille will help you meditate on what we have just said during your stay with us.

BROTHER JUDE

I understand, excellency. I do not mean to cause any trouble, but I just feel that we know enough to state that the shroud is authentic...! mean—

THE POPE

Brother Jude! If we knew as much, we would say as much.
We do not know as much. You may wish to consider why
so little of your work has been approved for publication.

BROTHER JUDE

I... I... as you wish, Your Excellency. I will not be writing anymore.

Brother Jude bows his head. He looks at his feet. The entourage reaches the end of the corridor where another impos ing door impedes their progress. The orderlies open the door. The Pope turns to Brother Jude and offers his ring. Brother Jude falls to his knees.

THE POPE

Good.

Brother Jude kisses the Pope's ring. The Pope walks through the doors, and they slam shut behind him. The heavy hasp clangs and locks, leaving the two friends on their knees. Cardinal DeVille puts his arm around his chastised friend's shoulder and helps Brother Jude to his feet.

CARDINAL DEVILLE

Don't take it so hard. Come on, Bill, we are going to my
favorite place in Rome for a repast.

BROTHER JUDE

Jack, I think I know how Galileo may have felt.

12. INT. CAPRI RESTAURANT—AFTERNOON 12

The elegant restaurant is half-filled with people and is thinning out as the lunch crowd finishes. Cardinal DeVille and Brother Jude are seated at the best table in the restaurant. Two waiters are clearing a lavish meal from the table. Another waiter approaches the table, pulls a bottle of wine from the ice bucket next to it, and pours the last of it into the two nearly empty glasses.

CARDINAL DEVILLE

Looks like the last of the wine. How about a cognac, Bill?

BROTHER JUDE

Nobody but you and my real brother, Clay, have called me
Bill for almost fifteen years, Jack.

Cardinal DeVille is only half-listening to Brother Jude. Cardinal
DeVille watches the waiter, Amelio, as he finishes pouring the wine.

CARDINAL DEVILLE (in Italian with subtitles)

Amelio, how about two of your special reserves

AMELIO

Very good, Father...and we have your favorite tiramisu today.

CARDINAL DEVILLE

We'll have two special reserves now, tiramisu and
two cappuccinos in a bit.

BROTHER JUDE

I don't know if I can—

CARDINAL DEVILLE (interrupting)

Of course, you can.

Cardinal DeVille dismisses Amelio with a wave of his hand.

CARDINAL DEVILLE (continuing)

Where you are going, the concept of cuisine has not entered
their Scottish minds!

Cardinal DeVille snatches his glass of wine and raises it in a toast.

CARDINAL DEVILLE (continuing)

Let's drink to your new life, Bill.

Brother Jude raises his glass. The glasses touch with the tintinnabulation
of fine crystal.

BROTHER JUDE
Thanks, Jack. I will have no such distractions to interrupt my
contemplations in Scotland.

The friends sip their wine together.

CARDINAL DEVILLE
Life is what you make it, that's for sure, Bill.

BROTHER JUDE
Oh, and I've pretty well messed up mine. Is that it, Jack?

CARDINAL DEVILLE
I didn't say that. I didn't say that at all, Bill. But you just did,
and I don't know why you feel that way.

BROTHER JUDE
Well, let's see—how about for starters, that nothing
has ever quite worked out the way I thought it should
and for a kicker, let's throw in that now I live in a little
cell day after day, getting nowhere. How's that?

Brother Jude looks deeply into his glass of wine. He takes another
long sip.

BROTHER JUDE (continuing)
You know what I'd like. I'd like for you to answer one question for me.
How did you get to be such a big shot in the Vatican anyway?

CARDINAL DEVILLE
As they used to say in our old neighborhood, fuhgiddaboutit — doan
worry 'bout it. Listen, you have the chance to start a great new life. Take
the opportunity with joy. Is your older brother, Clay, still near Edinburgh?
Because it's going to be important for you not to be in so much isolation
anymore.

BROTHER JUDE (quietly)
Yes, he is still there.

CARDINAL DEVILLE (laughingly)
So he's still clonin' around in Scotland.

BROTHER JUDE
That's not funny, Jack. I've been going through so much
for over a year now, it's like vuja de.

CARDINAL DEVILLE
Do you mean de ja vu?

BROTHER JUDE
No. I mean vuja de, the feeling that this has never happened before.

CARDINAL DEVILLE
So now you can make a joke, and it's okay, but I can't.
Is that the double standard that we're using?

BROTHER JUDE
The point is I need you to understand and
not joke around—that's the point, Jack.

CARDINAL DEVILLE
I know you do, Bill, and I'm always attuned to that.
You know that, don't you?

BROTHER JUDE
Yeah, I know. You're right, but it just feels like
I'm so alone at times. You know I can't promise you what
my meditations on all of this will produce.
I'm not sure they will be resolved to anyone's
satisfaction, even my own.

Amelio brings two special reserves and puts them on the table.

AMELIO
I'll have the tiramisu and the cappuccinos shortly, Father.

CARDINAL DEVILLE
Very good, Amelio. Thank you, no hurry.
Cardinal DeVille turns his attention back to Brother Jude.

CARDINAL DEVILLE (continuing)
Whatever happened to our resolution when we were kids?
Remember that saying in the fortune cookie we split?

BROTHER JUDE
Oh! Uh! "Simplicity of character is..."
CARDINAL DEVILLE (finishing the sentence)
"Is the natural result of profound thought."

BROTHER JUDE
Yeah, right...I attempted the profound thought part,
and I'm not sure what happened after that.

CARDINAL DEVILLE
I'd say, you are the furthest thing from simple that I know.
And that's not an insult at all in this context. I don't mean it
that way at all. It is more of a compliment to your intelligence.

They are both sipping the special reserves.

BROTHER JUDE
That means something coming from you, Jack. Thank you.

CARDINAL DEVILLE
I think I might know where you kind of might have gone off
track to some extent if you would permit me.

BROTHER JUDE
Please, I need all the help I can get.

CARDINAL DEVILLE

Unfortunately, it may not help you much at this point,
but for us to learn anything, we may be able to use it for others.

BROTHER JUDE

True enough. So get to it then...I'm listening.

CARDINAL DEVILLE

I don't think you had anyone to look up to and try to emulate.
I was very lucky in that regard. But for you, I don't know.
What do you think?

BROTHER JUDE

Oh, for sure! You are right on that point.
I never saw anyone I wanted to be like.

CARDINAL DEVILLE

I believe we are supposed to let people know who we
are so we can find the flaws in ourselves from their
observations of us and the feedback they give us.

BROTHER JUDE

That's all well and good in theory, but it's not long before
people abuse the information you let them have and start ridiculing,
laughing, mocking, and every other thing under the sun.

CARDINAL DEVILLE

That is a problem, no doubt, but being too isolated
and secretive is a bigger problem, I think. I want to say
this to you before we get too far afield. There's something
I never told you, and I don't want you to take it
the wrong way, but do you remember the
Jean Dixon book that came out, *A Gift of Prophecy*?

BROTHER JUDE

Naturally, I never read it.

CARDINAL DEVILLE
In the book, she gives a date that was somehow
connected to the Antichrist.

BROTHER JUDE
Okay.

CARDINAL DEVILLE
It was February 4, 1960.

BROTHER JUDE (shaking his head no several times)
My birthday! What, I'm the Antichrist now?

CARDINAL DEVILLE
I told you I didn't want you to take it the wrong way.
It was just something that struck me at the time.
Besides, you weren't born in the Middle East where
Dixon said this was to have taken place. I just want you to
know that you have always struck me as the
type of person who, even though he knew the
tremendous power of evil that could be unleashed,
would still open Pandora's Jar.

BROTHER JUDE
And why not, Jack? The power of good is even stronger, and you know it.

CARDINAL DEVILLE
Yes, but that doesn't mean we don't have to be careful, Bill.
We can't force the hand of God. It has to be His will, not ours.
That jar has to remain shut until such time as He opens it, if ever.
If nothing else, this life may only be a testing ground to see which people
are the ones who would dare to open such a jar.
Did you ever think of that?

BROTHER JUDE
What are we supposed to do? Sit around and play fiddlesticks the way
most people just screw up their lives? (more)

BROTHER JUDE (continued)
At least, we have dedicated and consecrated our lives
to something bigger than just ourselves and our lusts.

CARDINAL DEVILLE
Waiting, Bill. Waiting is doing something.

BROTHER JUDE
Waiting? Waiting for what?

CARDINAL DEVILLE
Waiting for Him. That's what we are to do.

BROTHER JUDE
I can't do that anymore—I must do more than just that.

CARDINAL DEVILLE
Bill! What more can we do?

BROTHER JUDE
I don't know, but something is better than nothing.
And his eminence tells me I can't write the truth about the shroud.

CARDINAL DEVILLE
You know, speaking about people to emulate...
if there is anyone better to emulate, I don't know who it would be.
His excellency was very tender in his rebuke.

BROTHER JUDE
And I thought he was a pompous a—

CARDINAL DEVILLE
Don't say that!

Cardinal DeVille glances to see if anyone heard and gives Brother Jude
a very disturbed look.

BROTHER JUDE (whispering)
Yeah, all right, I won't say it out loud—but
I never did like that ring-kissing business.
(more)

BROTHER JUDE (continued)
It's the reason I didn't take my final vows for the priesthood.

CARDINAL DEVILLE
You can criticize the man all you want, but he's an
absolute genius—and that's in addition to his obvious
spiritual qualities! He has forgotten more than you, and I ever knew.

BROTHER JUDE
Jack, the way these people treat me, I feel like I have
forgotten more than I know. And now you have started the
"Our Father who art on earth," and we are not going there, Jack.

CARDINAL DEVILLE
All right. *Pacem in terris*...happy birthday, Bill.

The friends pick up their glasses and toast.

CARDINAL DEVILLE (continuing)
Here's to a new and better life for you— that's the important thing.

Amelio brings the deserts and cappuccinos.
AMELIO
Will there be anything else, Father?

CARDINAL DEVILLE
No. Go ahead and put that on the usual tab—with
the usual gratuity.

AMELIO
Very well, Father. Thank you very much.
Amelio takes the empty reserve glasses and leaves.

CARDINAL DEVILLE
You have to admit that you have been somewhat fanatical
in your inquiries. You have to, at least, admit that, Bill.
And you pretty much promised His Holiness that you
would stop all this shroud business.

BROTHER JUDE
Business! Business! The shroud is not a business— there's
nothing for sale. I am not a capitalist.

I am not doing this for profit. And I am not fanatical. To say that is
ridiculous.

CARDINAL DEVILLE
You have studied it for years, and you know that three
different tests in 1988 proved that the Shroud is only
seven hundred or eight hundred years old.

BROTHER JUDE
No. That's incorrect. The same test was performed three times.
The shroud sample was cut into three sections and sent to three different
labs. That is not the same as three different tests, Jack.

CARDINAL DEVILLE
Okay, I'll concede to that, but...
BROTHER JUDE
And it turns out the tests were not done on the cloth alone.

CARDINAL DEVILLE
What do you mean by that?

BROTHER JUDE
One brilliant scientist finally figured out that the bacteria
in a cloth that old throw the tests off because the bacteria
are being tested at the same time. Obviously, all the bacteria
are not two thousand years old.
(more)

BROTHER JUDE (continued)
And another brilliant scientist, a housewife in America no less, figured that the cloth must have been repaired by the nuns with new cloth, which threw off the carbon 14 tests.

CARDINAL DEVILLE
I was not aware of that.

BROTHER JUDE
Yeah, there is a lot you aren't aware of—like the fire in fifteen thirty-two in the cathedral—

CARDINAL DEVILLE
Yeah, I know about that. I'm not altogether—

BROTHER JUDE
Fine! You know how hot the fire was then.

CARDINAL DEVILLE
How would I know that? What are you—

BROTHER JUDE
The holes in the shroud were made by molten silver.

CARDINAL DEVILLE
I know that! It is common knowledge.

BROTHER JUDE
Silver melts at nine hundred and sixty degrees.

CARDINAL DEVILLE
So?

BROTHER JUDE
So—it turns out that if any cloth is subjected to more than two hundred degrees, it throws off any carbon 14 test.

CARDINAL DEVILLE
All right, so I didn't know that, okay?

BROTHER JUDE
Did you know that the method of stitching is a method used
for only a short period of time almost two thousand years ago?

CARDINAL DEVILLE
Interesting!

BROTHER JUDE
Did you know that the face is on both sides of the cloth
and not in the middle?

CARDINAL DEVILLE
Where are we going with this?

BROTHER JUDE
We already know that the image is a negative that becomes
a positive when photographed with negative film.

CARDINAL DEVILLE
Certainly, that's how all this goofy stuff started in 1898
when the first photo of the shroud was taken.

BROTHER JUDE
Right! Guess what? The image was not painted on the cloth.

CARDINAL DEVILLE
I never thought it was painted on.

BROTHER JUDE
The head is perfecdy symmetrical. Human or should I say
beings that are only human are not perfectly symmetrical.

CARDINAL DEVILLE
Continue.

BROTHER JUDE

The only way that the image on the shroud could
have been formed is by His body dematerializing
through the shroud.

CARDINAL DEVILLE

The only way! That is patently absurd.

BROTHER JUDE

Oh! Whoa, now you don't believe in the resurrection!

CARDINAL DEVILLE

Don't be ridiculous.

BROTHER JUDE

Then what the devil are we arguing about, Jack? If this was
not Yahshua of Nazareth, the Christ, then it was someone
else who died the same way with the same nail points,
the thorns, the scourging, and the same spear wound.
Is that what you would rather believe?

CARDINAL DEVILLE

Of course not! Calm down, Bill.

BROTHER JUDE

But, but, but...the real key, Jack, the real key is in the thumbs.
In the thumbs. You know, the computer graphics
that shows the three-dimensional body?

CARDINAL DEVILLE

Yes, I saw that on TV.

BROTHER JUDE

Well, Jack, the thumbs on each hand are tucked under
the four fingers of each hand, and the hands
are resting on the stomach.

CARDINAL DEVILLE
Yeah.

BROTHER JUDE
Yeah, and yet the thumbs show up on the three-dimensional image.
So how does anyone explain that, Jack?

Cardinal DeVilles eyebrows are furrowed. He shakes his head in both
wonderment and irritation.

CARDINAL DEVILLE
So you know things others don't know. Why don't we all know these
things if they are so set in stone as you portray them?

BROTHER JUDE
Yeah, why don't we all know?
The fact is that you haven't taken the time to know.
The fact is that people believe what they are told to
believe by the so-called authorities,
and everyone is afraid to think otherwise.
They wind up thinking they know what just ain't so.
If I wanted to be rude, Jack, I could say you don't know, Jack.

CARDINAL DEVILLE
I appreciate you not being rude, Bill.

BROTHER JUDE
Listen, Jack, I did not want to believe what I learned
about those three tests. Those tests should have yielded
closer results than they did. There should not have
been a one-hundred-and-thirty-year discrepancy.

CARDINAL DEVILLE
I don't understand—

BROTHER JUDE

Carbon 14 tests are more precise than 1 thought.
The discrepancy proves two different fabrics were mixed.
One lab getting more of one fabric than the other—
that explains the discrepancy.

CARDINAL DEVILLE

This is all very interesting and also very immaterial.
You are just going to have to wait until—

BROTHER JUDE

I don't have to wait for a damn thing, Jack.
I've taken steps that will prove that I am right.
(more)

BROTHER JUDE (continued)

I'll show you and the world who knows what!

CARDINAL DEVILLE

Bill, please calm down. You're taking this much too much—

BROTHER JUDE

It won't be just me writing about it—it will be flesh and—
Brother Jude's face is scarlet. His eyes bulge out.

BROTHER JUDE (continuing) Blood—

He rips off his tight Roman collar and collapses unconscious
onto the table. Cardinal DeVille jolts up and rushes
to the aid of his friend.

13. INT. BROTHER JUDE'S BEDROOM CLOISTER CELL—NIGHT 13

The sparse monastery room is shown in sepia tones as we enter into
Brother Jude's dream world reenactment of his crime.
Brother Jude is standing in his room, and he puts his hood over his
head and opens the door and then steps into the corridor.

14. INT. MONASTERY CORRIDOR—CONTINUING 14

He hunches over. His hood over his head and his hands hidden in the folds of his robe, he quickly and quietly walks down the deserted corridor.

15. INT. SHROUD OF TURIN DISPLAY CHAPEL—CONTINUING 15

He walks into the chapel. He looks around. He walks to the rack of votive candles. Some are burning, and some are not.

He takes a wooden stick from the dispenser and lights it. He stuffs a rag under and around the candles. He lights all the candles. He takes a few of the candles that are swimming in molten wax and pours the wax over the rags. The rags start to burn, and he hurriedly retraces his steps back towards his bedroom cloister cell. He passes the crucifix that he used in opening scenes. The crucifix is hanging properly until he passes it and exits the chapel into the corridor. The crucifix slides with a grating sound upside down.

16. INT. MONASTERY CORRIDOR—CONTINUING 16

Brother Jude stops in his tracks. He listens. He hears no other sound. Smoke is starting to fill the chapel. Quickly, he continues down the corridor and returns to his cell.

Brother Jude arrives at his cell door. He enters his room.

17. INT. BROTHER JUDE'S BEDROOM CELL—CONTINUING 17

Brother Jude flips his hood down, checks the evidence bag in his cloak, and puts the one latex glove in his hand. As the fire alarm clangs, he snaps the last pull of the latex glove onto his wrist.

18. INT VATICAN INFIRMARY ROOM—DAY 18

Dr. Scarfidi snaps on his latex glove. Brother Jude is lying on the hospital bed with an oxygen hose in his nose. Brother Jude begins to stir as he comes to consciousness.

BROTHER JUDE
Oh my God! What have I done? Brother Adrian!
What happened to Brother Adrian?

Cardinal DeVille puts down the black book of his office that he was reading. He stands and goes to Brother Jude's aid.

CARDINAL DEVILLE
You are okay, Bill. You're in the Vatican Infirmary.
Can you hear me? The doctor is here, and he is coming.

Dr. Scarfidi approaches the bed.

BROTHER JUDE
Oh, Jack, I'm so sorry...

CARDINAL DEVILLE
Now, Bill, take it easy—

DR. SCARFIDI
Well, well, Brother Jude, I'm Doctor Scarfidi,
who welcomes you back to the land of the living.

BROTHER JUDE
What do you mean by that?

DR. SCARFIDI
You've been unconscious for three days.

BROTHER JUDE (whispering)
Three days and three nights...

DR. SCARFIDI
Yes, but the good news is that we have done all
the tests on you, and you are physically exhausted
and not much more, thank God.

CARDINAL DEVILLE
You better start taking care of yourself, Bill! Doctor,
when will Brother Jude be able to transfer to
one of the private dorm rooms?

DR. SCARFIDI
Very soon, I should think. Maybe two more days for observation.
So, Brother Jude, if you require anything,
here is the button to summon a nurse. Okay?

BROTHER JUDE
Very good. Thank you, Doctor. Thank you very much.
Doctor Scarfidi exits the room, leaving the two
friends alone together.Cardinal DeVille pulls his chair
close to Brother Jude's bed and sits down
to talk to Brother Jude.

CARDINAL DEVILLE
As soon as you are out of here and into one of our rooms,
I want you to talk to someone.

BROTHER JUDE
Jack, I am getting the feeling you want me to talk
to one of your head doctors... is that it?

CARDINAL DEVILLE
Don't be reading my mind—but you guessed
right— but she is a theologian as well as a
psychiatrist who works right here in the Vatican.

BROTHER JUDE She?
CARDINAL DEVILLE Yes, she—Doctor Darcy Sol.

BROTHER JUDE
Really? I am familiar with some of her ideas.
I would like to talk with her—

CARDINAL DEVILLE
I thought you would have heard of her. She is very good,
you know—try to make good use of her talents—the price is
right too—we are very fortunate to have these resources
at our beck and call.

Brother Jude's eyes begin to close. He coughs and looks like he is about to fall asleep.

CARDINAL DEVILLE (continuing)
I'm leaving you to rest now, Bill. Just relax,
everything is taken care of.

19. INT. DR. SOL'S OFFICE—DAY 19

Dr. Darcy Sol, about thirty-five years old, sits at her desk. A pad of paper is on the desk and she is holding a pen. Brother Jude sits opposite her. He leans closer to her.

BROTHER JUDE
I very much appreciate this opportunity to meet you in person.
I've heard a lot about you, and I have read a number of your papers...
I could not have dreamed that I would be sitting here with you,
and I am really flattered that I am so important—

DR. SOL
Brother Jude, you should know how important you are by now!
Everyone wants to see you healthy and feeling like your old self,
so please, let's begin with the assumption that I know nothing
about you and now you tell me something.

BROTHER JUDE
I can assume that you know about the fire and all that?

DR. SOL
Yes, that was big news. I heard what the Pope said about you too, so if that
is where you would like to begin—

BROTHER JUDE
I guess I put myself under a lot of pressure concerning
the authenticity of the shroud. I'm over that now.
All's well or will be with that matter...
what I would like to do is ask some questions about
a philosophical issue that we are both very interested in.

DR. SOL
Which one is that?

BROTHER JUDE
I mean these are just silly things and have nothing to do with my
condition, except that they have interfered with my responsibilities—

DR. SOL
If these questions have interfered with your responsibilities,
they are not silly—so that seems to be a good place to begin...fire away.
Oh, I'm sorry—no pun intended.

BROTHER JUDE
No pun taken.

DR. SOL
That's funny. I like that, or should I say that's punny?
\Humor is an important part of mental health, brother,
and I want you to know that.

BROTHER JUDE
Does that mean you can laugh at your jokes?

DR. SOL
Most definitely, brother—please continue.

BROTHER JUDE
Okay—firing away now...I understand you have
a degree in theology.

DR. SOL

I studied at Oxford if that counts around here...

BROTHER JUDE

This has been bothering me for a very long time...
it's like an obsession with me. It concerns the conflict
between science and faith—and in particular the issue of cloning.
Have you been watching this issue like I have?

DR. SOL

Certainly—please continue.

BROTHER JUDE

My question is about human cloning or the cloning of
a human being and the philosophical ramifications—

DR. SOL

Human cloning is banned by the scientific community,
but the potential exists and poses questions that interest me as well.

BROTHER JUDE

I am very confused about this issue, and 1 would very much like to hear
your thoughts about it.

DR. SOL

Well.. .it is quite a challenge, and I like to think of it this way.
Everyone knows the scripture that says,
"Faith without works is dead," but the rest of that passage says,
"Even as the body without the spirit is dead."

BROTHER JUDE

Yes—I know the passage well.

DR. SOL

So, continuing, we know a body without a
spirit is a dead body, don't we?

BROTHER JUDE
Yes, I follow that line of reasoning.

DR. SOL
This is consistent with the teaching in Genesis where it says
God took dust of the ground and breathed into it—the
word breathe is the word for spirit—and man became a living soul.
When matter and spirit are put together, man becomes not just a mixture
of the two but a third entity called a living soul.

BROTHER JUDE
So what you seem to be saying is that the word man
is synonymous with a living soul.

DR. SOL (nodding)
So in Ecclesiastes where it says that the body returns
to dust and the spirit returns to God from whence it came,
that is exactly what happens, and consequently there is no
more soul and no more man...
I like to use the analogy of the water molecule.

BROTHER JUDE
The water molecule... H2O?

DR. SOL
Yes, you have two things making a third thing.
When the hydrogen and oxygen are together,
they make the water molecule. When they are taken apart,
there is no more water.

BROTHER JUDE
But the two parts remain...So when we die, there is no more soul, no
living soul, no more man as such?

DR. SOL
Exactly. There continues to be matter and spirit individually.

BROTHER JUDE

That's funny. I have often used a similar analogy
when counseling married couples...so just how
did this immortal soul stuff ever get started?

DR. SOL

Plato—

BROTHER JUDE

Ah, Plato! I think I know where you are going with this.
Continue, please.

DR. SOL

Plato looked at the matter of a living man and the matter
of a dead man and concluded they were the same matter—
but something was missing, so he concluded that
something was immaterial, and he named it soul.
He called the invisible part the soul.

BROTHER JUDE

This is what the Bible calls the spirit and—

DR. SOL

And so the discrepancy begins!

BROTHER JUDE

So...if I am following correctly, according to Dr. Sol,
the spirit is immortal and goes back to God—

DR. SOL

And not the soul—you understand my thinking.

BROTHER JUDE

Of course, Jesus said, "Into thy hands I commend my spirit,"
not "my soul." Why have I never heard a sermon like this?

DR. SOL

Why, indeed? I can tell you because you have studied the Bible.
In fact, you seem to know it better than most priests I talk to.
If you try to tell this to people who have not studied,
it goes right over their heads, and as far as most in the seminaries,
they have been told so many other things by men that they
have trouble when God says it so simply.

BROTHER JUDE

Because of your last name, you naturally fell into this study.
Is that what happened?

DR. SOL

I am sure that had something to do with it.

BROTHER JUDE

What are your thoughts concerning the resurrection then—

DR. SOL

In the resurrection, God would miraculously reunite
the same spirit with the same body, thus, as the Psalm says,
"restoring" my soul. Recreating the same water molecule,
so to speak. (more)

DR. SOL (continued)

In reincarnation, if there is such a thing, the body would be different,
but the spirit the same. So a different water molecule...

BROTHER JUDE

Have you put this into writing anywhere?

DR. SOL

Perhaps you don't understand this as well as I do yet, but
around here, one has to be careful not to step on Superman's cape.

BROTHER JUDE

I'm glad I never became a priest.

DR. SOL
Why? You would have been a good one, I think.

BROTHER JUDE
I was just thinking that if I had given sermon after sermon week
after week and then heard you say what you just did,
I would have thoughts in the back of my mind that many
of the sermons I gave were simply wrong, and I may not have
been able to face that, and so I would be thinking
of ways to make you wrong instead of just learning
and admitting my mistake.

DR. SOL
In case you are wondering, we are getting to
the answer of your question. I want you to look at
Zechariah chapter 12, verse 1. It says God forms the
spirit in man. So of course, we don't know exactly
when God forms the breath or spirit in a baby,
but this scripture does tell us that He does that.

BROTHER JUDE
I remember considering this in connection with the question
of when does a fetus or embryo become a human being.
So we don't really know exactly when God forms the
spirit in the living tissue of the fetus.

DR. SOL
Right. So I said all this to say that if God forms a human
spirit in a cloned body, then he or she would be human.
If God does not form a human spirit in the clone,
then it would not be human no matter how it looked.
You know the saying, "Appearances can be deceiving."

BROTHER JUDE
I think I understand. You are saying that the clone
could be an animal and not human. Is that it?

DR. SOL

Yes, that could happen. I'm not saying it would happen.
I don't know what would happen. It would be interesting to know,
but now they are already outlawing human cloning.

BROTHER JUDE

Assuming it looked human, would there be any way
we could tell the difference?

DR. SOL

I can only guess that if it were only an animal,
it should not be able to speak or communicate the way we do.
I mean in abstract symbols, words if you will.

BROTHER JUDE

That makes sense. This has been most helpful. I think this
has been enough for me for our first day, if you don't mind.

DR. SOL

I understand. Why don't we schedule three quarters of an
hour every Thursday at 3:00 p.m.? Would that be all right?

BROTHER JUDE

That would be fine. I will be around for some months before
I relocate to Scotland near my brother.

DR. SOL

Great. We will talk about that next time.
You may leave the door open if you will on your way out.

BROTHER JUDE

Thank you so much for your time and concern.
You have made me feel very much better.

20. INT. LIMOUSINE—AFTERNOON 20

SUPER—October 6, 1993, Edinburgh, Scotland

The luxurious car quietly moves through the Scottish countryside. The chauffeur is quiet until Brother Jude speaks.

BROTHER JUDE
Can we stop at the International Cloning Institute
before you take me to the Rosslyn Chapel?

CHAUFFEUR
Very well, brother. It's not far out of the way.

21. EXT. INTERNATIONAL CLONING INSTITUTE CONTINUING 21

Brother Jude exits the vehicle to enter the International Cloning Institute.

22. INT. INSIDE INSTITUTE—CONTINUING 22

The reception area seems to be all glass with views of the verdant countryside. A receptionist sits at her desk.

BROTHER JUDE
Dr. Adams, please.

RECEPTIONIST
Is he expecting you, sir?

BROTHER JUDE
Please tell him Brother Jude is here.
He has been waiting for me for five months.

RECEPTIONIST
Oh, you are his brother, aren't you? Welcome.
I will let him know immediately.

BROTHER JUDE
Thank you.

Before Brother Jude wanders far from the desk.

RECEPTIONIST
Sir, you may walk down that hall in front of you.
Dr. Adams is already on his way to meet you.

Brother Jude walks down a hallway and soon meets with his brother, Clay Adams. Clay is trim and vigorous despite the fact that he is in his early forties with gray and thinning hair. The brothers embrace.

CLAY ADAMS
Come into my office before we talk about anything.

BROTHER JUDE
It's so good to see you after so many years.

CLAY ADAMS
It's great to see you. Everything went fine. I'll tell you about it. This way.

The two enter Dr. Adams' office.

23. INT DR. ADAMS' OFFICE—CONTINUING 23

CLAY ADAMS
The birth was last night, just as you said it would be,
October fifth...how did you guess something like that, Bill?

BROTHER JUDE
It's a long story, Clay. We don't need to go into the details.
The key was that you told me on the phone that the
cloning was successful on December twenty-fifth.

CLAY ADAMS
Anyway, everything went fine. She's beautiful.

BROTHER JUDE
What? She?

CLAY ADAMS
Hey, come on, I'm only kidding.

BROTHER JUDE
Don't do that! You know I am nervous enough about this.

CLAY ADAMS
He's fine. He is beautiful. Everything went great.
He seems perfectly normal. In fact, maybe more than normal.

BROTHER JUDE
What do you mean by that? You're scaring me again.

CLAY ADAMS
He did not cry...he laughed at me within the first
minute of birth. I would say that that is more than normal.
His name has already been officially registered
as you requested, Joshua Christian Adams.

BROTHER JUDE
And the circumcision?

CLAY ADAMS
Already scheduled for the eighth day. Will you stop worrying?
I am doing everything we discussed.

BROTHER JUDE
What about the surrogate?

CLAY ADAMS
Believe it or not—because I don't—her name is Maria.
She has been paid in full and knows that she is
to have nothing further to do with the child.

BROTHER JUDE
I suppose her husband's name was Joseph.

CLAY ADAMS

That I don't know. In fact, I don't think she is married.

BROTHER JUDE

Okay. Well, I have to be on my way.
So if anything comes up, you know where to reach me.

CLAY ADAMS

Let me walk you to the front.

BROTHER JUDE

Yes, I will be calling regularly

FADE OUT:

24. EXT. CLAY ADAMS' HOUSE—DAY 24

FADE IN:

SUPER—Twelve Years Later

The sound of ringing is heard, but it is not a phone but rather the doorbell being rung by Brother Jude. Clay Adams answers the door.

CLAY ADAMS

Bill, it's so good to finally see you again.
Gosh, it has been a year and a half. Hasn't it?

BROTHER JUDE

Yeah, it was just before our last beloved Pope died.

CLAY ADAMS

Come in. Come in. Josh has been ready, but when you
didn't show up on time—I am not sure what he is
doing at the moment. Are you running late now?

25. INT. INSIDE THE CLAY HOME—DAY 25

BROTHER JUDE

No, no, I have plenty of time. In fact, we can talk a bit before Josh and I
leave for the conference.

CLAY ADAMS

That's something new. I am sure happy about that.
Let me pour you a drink.

BROTHER JUDE

No, no… well, okay, maybe a small one. Where is Josh?
I just want to say hi.

Clay Adams pours two drinks.

CLAY ADAMS

He may have gone out back.

BROTHER JUDE

I will just say hi and be right back, and then we can talk.

Brother Jude walks to the back of the house and looks out the kitchen
window to see Josh making twelve mud sparrows. As he forms the last one,
Josh claps his hands and raises both hands into the air, and they come alive
and fly away. Brother Jude, with shock on his face, as Josh then turns and
looks into the window to see Brother Jude and Josh, smiling at him.

Brother Jude turned with a smile on his face to return to Clay Adams
and took the drink from Clay's hand.

CLAY ADAMS

I must say, you look exceptionally well. Here's to all of us.
The glasses touch. They each sip, and Clay goes to light a cigar.

BROTHER JUDE

How has Josh been doing with the tutors?

CLAY ADAMS

He learns everything. And I do mean everything they know,
and I have to get another and another and on and on.

And on top of that, he tries to correct some things
he thinks are wrong, and I have had some tutors up
and quit on us just like that.

BROTHER JUDE
Who do you have teaching him the Bible?

CLAY ADAMS
I have priests, rabbis, ministers—the whole catastrophe.

BROTHER JUDE
Has he done anything like—anything like...

CLAY ADAMS
Like what?

BROTHER JUDE
Like supernatural in front of you?

CLAY ADAMS
No. Why?

Clay sips from his glass.

CLAY ADAMS (continuing)
But look at this piece of furniture he made from scratch.
You know he didn't have any help from me on something like this.

BROTHER JUDE
That is beautiful.

CLAY ADAMS
He is amazing, Bill. I just hope all this works out
the way you think it will.
(more)

CLAY ADAMS (continued)
I have been meaning to talk to you for the last year and

a half since the new Pope was elected, what do you think?
Are you on better terms with him than the last one?

BROTHER JUDE

Not really. He seems all right, but there is no
progress as far as my personal interests.

CLAY ADAMS

I know you had to be hoping, but nothing yet?

BROTHER JUDE

Not yet, and it doesn't really look very promising.

CLAY ADAMS

Do you remember the prophecies of Malachi
that we discussed some years ago?

BROTHER JUDE

Of course, I remember.

CLAY ADAMS

Is that in the Bible?

BROTHER JUDE

No, it's not that Malachi. This one was a monk in the middle ages who
listed some popes into the future with a short phrase about each one.

CLAY ADAMS

Right. Yeah, I remember Pope John the twenty- third was a pastor and
mariner or something like that, and he came from Venice.

BROTHER JUDE

That's right. You got it.

CLAY ADAMS

That almost could be a self-fulfilling prophecy since
I presume all the cardinals know about the prophecy. Right?

BROTHER JUDE
I am sure they do.

CLAY ADAMS
What about since then? I have lost track.

BROTHER JUDE
We had John Paul I that was said to be of the half moon.
It sounds like fourteen or fifteen days. It actually turned out
to be thirty-three days. That does sound like a short time
and not easily self-fulfilling. Although...

CLAY ADAMS
Although what?

BROTHER JUDE
I was going to say some think he may have been poisoned,
but nothing ever came out about that.

CLAY ADAMS
What about John Paul II?

BROTHER JUDE
He was said to be "of the labor of the sun." It turns out he was
born on the day of a solar eclipse, May 18, 1920, and was buried
on the day of a solar eclipse in April 2005. The second part of that,
the burial, could have been planned as it was delayed more than a few
days after his death. But his birthday would not have been known by
many when he was elected. His role with Fatima and the downfall of
communism is well known.

CLAY ADAMS
Unbelievable!

BROTHERJUDE
It really is, I think.

CLAY ADAMS

What about this Benedict the sixteenth?

BROTHER JUDE

His phrase is "gloria olivae" or something like that.

CLAY ADAMS

What do the experts make of that one?

BROTHER JUDE

Good question. The olive branch naturally is the sign of peace.
This could take different paths, though. Some
thought he could reunite the Protestants to Holy Mother Church
in this ecumenical movement. Others thought the Muslims
might come around to a more peaceful coexistence with the Church,
at least. You know Mohammed's daughter's name was Fatima?

CLAY ADAMS

I certainly didn't know that one.

BROTHER JUDE

Benedict is the first German Pope in almost a thousand years.
One of his first acts was to put his foot in his mouth as far as
the Muslims were concerned. He probably just made a
mistake, nothing intentional, but that does not really
help matters much. Some writers years ago had speculated
that this Pope could have some Jewish blood. But again,
nothing like this has come from reliable sources yet.
It is possible, we just don't know. But there is
one overwhelming significance to this Pope.

CLAY ADAMS

What is that, pray tell?

BROTHER JUDE

He is the second to the last Pope in the prophecies of Malachi.

CLAY ADAMS
Really? What does it say about the last one?

BROTHER JUDE
"Peter of Rome." Some think he will take the name
Peter the Second, but that would really be self-fulfilling.

CLAY ADAMS
I just realized that the age of this Pope also causes some
concern about the coming of the last Pope in the prophecies.

BROTHER JUDE
That's right. Even if he lasted to ninety, that would be about 2017...
One thing is for sure, the last Pope in this day and age will not
be taking the name of Pope Innocent. I guess things will
kind of peter out after this last Pope—hey, ha-ha-ha,
that is funny, if I do say so myself. Maybe these are the end times.

CLAY ADAMS
Well, I like your humor, and I agree with you. I think we are
in the end times, even if the last days were one-thousand-year
days and started at Pentecost itself. Believe me, I read
and reread your lengthy letter to me years ago that the
"last days" began two thousand years ago and involve one
thousand days and should not be confused with
the end times as listed in the Bible.

BROTHER JUDE
That is a technical point, and I think we are on the
morning of the third day. Speaking of which,
Josh and I had better be leaving for the conference.
I think we had better track him down. He may need to
clean up a bit from what I saw. Josh enters the room.

JOSHUA
Let there be light, Uncle Jude. I am already
cleaned up and all ready to go.

Josh runs to his uncle, Brother Jude, who picks Josh off his feet and hugs him.

BROTHER JUDE
And there was light.

Brother Jude places Josh back on his feet.

JOSHUA
I missed you so much, Uncle Jude.

BROTHER JUDE
I know. I missed you both so much also. I promise
I will never go a year and a half again without seeing
you one way or the other. Okay?

CLAY ADAMS
You ought to get going—the car is waiting—

JOSHUA
I wouldn't miss this for all the tea in China. Let's go.

BROTHER JUDE
Clay, wish your son happy twelfth birthday because
he will be twelve by the time we get back.

CLAY ADAMS
That's right. Happy birthday, Josh. We will do
something when you return. All right?

JOSHUA
This conference is the best birthday present
I have ever received. Everything else will just be
icing on the cake, I guess one would say.

CLAY ADAMS
I am so glad you are happy with something out

of the ordinary and not upset. You, guys, have a great time, and I will see you when you return in a few days.

JOSHUA
Goodbye, Father.

The two head for the door.

26. EXT. THEOLOGICAL CONFERENCE BUILDING— DAY 26

Brother Jude and Josh are getting out of a limo to enter the conference building.

SUPER—Theological Conference

27. INT. INSIDE CONFERENCE BUILDING CONTINUING 27

BROTHER JUDE
I have our badges, which allow us to go to any
and all of the lectures. Some may have a different
colored badge, which means they are only allowed
to attend certain lectures and not others.

JOSHUA
I understand, Uncle Jude. I like that. We can go to any one we want.

BROTHER JUDE
Oh, look! I want you to meet an old friend of mine,
Dr. Darcy Sol. She looks like she is just saying goodbye to someone,
and you can meet her without intruding.

JOSHUA
I want to meet all your friends, Uncle.
They walk toward Dr. Sol until they meet.

BROTHER JUDE
Dr. Sol, I would love for you to meet my nephew,
Joshua Adams. Josh, this is Dr. Darcy Sol, a very distinguished
and well-known psychiatrist—should I say inter alia—theologian.

JOSHUA
I am so pleased to meet you, Dr. Sol. You may call me Josh, if you like.

DR. SOL
Then I shall call you Josh, and I am so happy to meet you.

The two shake hands.

DR. SOL (continuing)
Brother Jude, it has been at least ten years.
It is so good to see you.

BROTHER JUDE
You have an excellent memory because it has been twelve years,
and my brother Clays son was born just after I left Rome to
go to Rosslyn Chapel. Josh will be twelve on the last day of this
conference. That is how I remember.

DR. SOL
And how have you been?

BROTHER JUDE
It could not be better for me unless I were living with
Josh and my brother, Clay.

DR. SOL
And this fine young man, I see, is wearing a badge for the conference
no less. Aren't you a little young for a conference like this, Josh?

BROTHER JUDE
I got special permission for Josh to attend, and
it was only because of his special qualifications, I assure you.

Also, Josh has promised not to be any hindrance to the attendees.
Isn't that right, Josh?

JOSHUA
That is correct, Uncle Jude.

DR. SOL
You must be very special, indeed, and I look forward
to seeing you both during the conference,
but I don't want to be late for my first lecture that I am giving.

BROTHER JUDE
We understand perfectly. Please don't be late.
We will catch that lecture another day as I noticed that it repeats.

Dr. Sol begins to leave, waving goodbye to them both.

JOSHUA
Goodbye, I am pleased I met you.

BROTHER JUDE
We don't want to be late either.

The session I had seen in our program was on the trinity in room 103.
Should we go to that one?

JOSHUA
Oh yes! Let's go.

The two hurriedly walk toward the lecture rooms.

28. INT OUTSIDE THE LECTURE ROOM—DUSK 28

BROTHER JUDE
How did you like your first day?

JOSHUA
It was great. Did you like it?

BROTHER JUDE
Very much. What do you say we go to dinner at our hotel?
Hit the hay early and get to our first lecture
on time tomorrow morning?

JOSHUA
Let's eat. I'm hungry.

BROTHER JUDE
You know on the third day, the last day of the conference,
we have to leave a little early to catch our plane.

JOSHUA
You told me on the plane on the way here.

They walk to exit the building.

BROTHER JUDE
I just wanted to be sure you remembered.

JOSHUA
I remember everything, Uncle Jude.

BROTHER JUDE
Good. Because there is nothing worse than forgetting.

JOSHUA
I just wish we could have gone to all the lectures instead
of having to pick some.

BROTHER JUDE
I know, and I am going to let you pick two-thirds of the
ones we attend tomorrow. How's that? Will that be fair?

JOSHUA
Yes, I like that.

BROTHER JUDE

You asked some very good questions today. I am proud of you.

They look at each other with big smiles. They go through the doors, exit the building.

29. INT. CONFERENCE BUILDING—AFTERNOON 29

SUPER—The Last Day of the Conference, Thursday, 3:00 PM

Brother Jude is frantically going from room to room look ing for Josh on the first floor to no avail.

30. INT. CLASSROOM—CONTINUING 30

Joshua is sitting with a group of seven scholars in a circle; Dr. Sol is one of the scholars.

JOSHUA

Yes, I know you are right that Scripture does not
tell us specifically what Judas told the High Priest
and the elders of the Sanhedrin, but I think
it must have been something like what I just said.

SCHOLAR ONE

Whoa. Wait a minute, just run the whole idea by us
one more time Josh, please.

JOSHUA

All right, let me say it this way—nowhere in the Bible does
it say to look for the sliver of the moon after the conjunction
of the sun and moon for there to be a beginning to the month. Right?

SCHOLAR TWO

Technically, that is correct, but it does say to observe the new moon.

JOSHUA

That's right, but I am saying that observing does not

necessarily mean seeing with one's eyes. There is a
specific scripture that says we walk by faith, not by sight.

SCHOLAR ONE
All right, let's say you are right that the new moon
is at the conjunction. Go ahead with what you are saying.

JOSHUA
So if the new moon is in the conjunction, then after two
nights of observing no moon in the sky, you know that a conjunction
took place. If Jesus had told only his disciples, knowing that those who
sat in Moses's seat would never accept it, then every month would be at
least one day off what it should be. The feasts with the annual Sabbaths
would all be off by at least one day and in some cases more than one day.
In the case of the Last Supper, it would have been just one day because
scripture tells us that the next day as they crucified Jesus, their high day
was approaching, the Passover. So they had to get him down from the
cross before sunset, or so they thought.

DR. SOL
So you are saying that Yahshua and the apostles were
actually celebrating the correct Passover day and that the nation
also celebrated the Passover but one day late.

JOSHUA
Exactly.

SCHOLAR THREE
You know that makes some sense to me because it would
answer some questions I have had.

SCHOLAR TWO
Like what?

SCHOLAR THREE
Remember the Bible tells us that they wanted to kill Jesus after
the money changers were thrown out of the temple,

but they decided to wait until the seven-day feast of Passover and the days of Unleavened Bread were finished because there were so many strangers in Jerusalem.

SCHOLAR FOUR
I certainly do remember that.

SCHOLAR THREE.
Whatever Judas did say on the night of the betrayal made them change their minds about waiting. They tore their garments and basically said, that's it, He has to die now. That always meant to me that Judas must have said more than just where to find Jesus on the night in question.

DR. SOL
I agree with that doctor.

SCHOLAR ONE
And they did the same thing every month.
They went out and declared that a new month started, and no one would have questioned it.
The error had to be hundreds of years old.

SCHOLAR TWO
Moses would have had to be doing it correctly.

SCHOLAR THREE
David also, because it is recorded in Scripture twice that David said tomorrow is the new moon.
He could not know ahead of time if he was doing it the way they were at the crucifixion.

SCHOLAR TWO
Yeah. Where is that in the Bible?

SCHOLAR THREE
Chronicles.

JOSHUA

So that is what I am saying. Judas walked in and told these
elders that he and the other apostles had just celebrated the
Passover on the correct day as outlined in Leviticus.
The elders had it scheduled for the next evening.

DR. SOL

Thus, making this a feast of the Jews instead of a feast
of Yahweh, just as John tells us in his Gospel.

SCHOLAR FIVE

I guess I might as well put my two cents in. Psalm 81 would
make better sense if this is correct because it says to blow the trumpet at
the new moon and on your feast at the full moon. If you started the new
moon late, the full moon would be past by the fourteenth or the fifteenth
of the month since the new moon are 29.5 days apart on average.

DR. SOL

So one-half of that is 14.75 days.

The Passover is on the fourteenth, and the high day in the fall feasts
designates the fifteenth.

SCHOLAR FIVE

The two perfect parameters

31. INT BUILDING—CONTINUING 31

Brother Jude is running up the stairs to the second-floor classrooms
and goes in one after another. He opens one closed classroom door to look
for Josh and interrupts lectures and apologizes.

BROTHER JUDE

I am sorry. Please forgive me. I didn't t mean to disrupt.

32. INT. JOSHUA'S CLASSROOM—CONTINUING 32

The scholars are deep in thought.

JOSHUA
All I am saying is that no righteous Jew would have taken
up a collection on the Sabbath day of worship for at least two reasons.
One is that the tithing of crops would have required work to
bring them to the synagogue. And two, since that is the last
day of the week, the seventh day, it would be the last fruits
and not the first fruits. And three, this would involve
materialism on their holy day.

DR. SOL
So that is the reason the apostles were told to lay up
in store their tithes unto the first day of the week.

JOSHUA
Right! And that would in no way indicate that the day of worship
had changed from Saturday to Sunday, the first
day of the week. Thus, they would not be mixing
gross materiality with spirituality.

Scholar two scratches his head.

33. INT. STAIRCASE—CONTINUING 33

Brother Jude is going downstairs to the first floor to the information
desk. He gets to the desk.

BROTHER JUDE
Are all the meeting rooms on the first and second floors?

RECEPTIONIST
Yes, of course… except for room 303.

BROTHER JUDE
303?

RECEPTIONIST
Yes. That is for the speakers and leaders of the conference only.

Brother Jude dashes for the elevator already completely out of breath. He pushes the "up" button impatiently and looks up at the clock on wall, but the elevator is not coming, so he takes to the stairs again.

34. INT. CLASSROOM—CONTINUING 34

JOSHUA

If you look at each scripture quoted by Jesus when
Satan tempted Him in the wilderness, He uses scriptures
that contain God's name, Yahweh, but it does not come
across clearly in the English because the word Lord
is used to replace the sacred name.

SCHOLAR ONE

That's correct. So you are saying that our Savior is using
His real name and the Father's name as a sword against
the adversary, to protect Himself and drive off the devil.

JOSHUA

That is exactly right.

35. INT. STAIRCASE—CONTINUING 35

Brother Jude exits the staircase to the third floor. He sees a long corridor and walks down it.

36. INT CLASSROOM—CONTINUING 36

JOSHUA

What I am asking is this—if the Holy Spirit is a person,
and the creed says Jesus was conceived by the Holy Spirit,
why wouldn't the Holy Spirit be His Father instead of the
Father being His Father?

The door bursts open. Brother Jude rushes into the room.

BROTHER JUDE

Oh, there you are. I am sorry for bursting in like this,
but we will be late for our plane if we do not leave immediately.
I am sorry for not knocking.

The participants are uneasy and talk amongst themselves.

BROTHER JUDE (continuing)

Josh, please come now.

Brother Jude realizes he has caused a stir and becomes deferential to the group.

BROTHER JUDE (continuing)

I am sorry to you all, but I must take him. I know you wanted to
answer all his questions, but we must go. Thank you for understanding.

Brother Jude and Josh rush from the room and close the door behind them. The camera stays on the circle of scholars.

SCHOLAR ONE

From the mouth of babes...

37. INT. ELEVATOR—AFTERNOON 37

Brother Jude and Josh are in the elevator going down to the first floor to exit building.

BROTHER JUDE

What are you doing to me? Why did you just leave me like that?

JOSHUA

I'm sorry. I got so absorbed. I heard Dr. Sol talking
to one of the other gentlemen, Benjamin I think his name was.
They were asking questions of each other, and I just followed them.
Before you knew it, I answered one of the questions for them,
and I found myself in that room with all of them.

BROTHER JUDE
All right. All right. It's my fault anyway. It's not that
I don't trust you. It's just that I am responsible for you.
Don't ever do that to me again. Please. Tell me you won't.

JOSHUA
I won't. I am sorry.

38. EXT. LEAVING BUILDING TO OUTSIDE CONTINUING 38

Josh looks up at Uncle Jude as they hurriedly walk toward a waiting limo.

JOSHUA
Uncle Jude, did you know my mother?

BROTHER JUDE
Uh... uh, get in. We are late.

They get into the limo.

JOSHUA
Well, did you?

BROTHER JUDE
Uh, no, not really. What did your father tell you?
He said you were adopted, right?

JOSHUA
Yes, but that is all he told me.

BROTHER JUDE
Well, in situations like that, the mother is often not even known.
Only the court has the records, and they are sealed.
It's just kind of a legal thing. You will understand
more as you get older, okay?

JOSHUA

Was father ever married?

BROTHER JUDE

No. You know that.

JOSHUA

Yes, I just thought that maybe my mother died in
childbirth and that Father didn't want to tell me.

BROTHER JUDE

No, Josh, that is not what happened. No one that
I know of ever knew your mother. Let's enjoy the ride.
We will be at the airport soon. Okay?

JOSHUA

Uncle Jude.

BROTHER JUDE

What?

JOSHUA

Sometimes I feel like you are my mother— or at least
like you are my second father.

BROTHER JUDE

I do too, Josh. I do too. And you know how much I love you.
And...by the way, happy birthday. I have something for you.

JOSHUA

You do? What?

BROTHER JUDE

Right here. Here it is. Open it.
Brother Jude pulls out a very expensive purple velvet case
containing the Holy Grail, which he will not tell Joshua.

BROTHER JUDE (continuing)
When you drink your grape juice at home I want you to use it,
and later you can drink wine from it. It is very special.

JOSHUA
Oh, this is so beautiful. Where did you get it?

BROTHER JUDE
Let's just say I followed some arcane clues, which others
had not properly interpreted, and found it in Rosslyn Chapel
where I am staying. Promise you will not tell anyone.
Just say it was a gift from me. I promise I will tell you
more about it when you are older. Can we agree on that?

JOSHUA
Oh yes, I will use it often, and I will keep it clean.

BROTHER JUDE
Very good. And when we get home, I am sure your
father will have a great party for just the three of us.
Josh smiles up at Uncle Jude.

FADE OUT

39. INT. HOME OF CLAY ADAMS' KITCHEN/DEN—DAY 39

FADE IN:

The kitchen/den is a large open room that looks out to the swimming pool. There is a large television screen on one wall and doors to two bathrooms or small locker rooms for changing into swimming suits. There is a long island with a sink at the end that is a few feet from the opposite wall where there are ovens, two more sinks, a preparation area, and cabinets. There are six high chairs with backs around the Italian marble island that doubles as an eating table or for family meetings. A wireless telephone in a cradle is mounted on the wall in easy reach from the table. A large fireplace and well-stocked bar is opposite the glass doors and glass wall that overlooks the pool. There are a few couches and stuffed chairs scattered around the room.

The phone on the wall is ringing.

SUPER—2023, Eighteen Years Later

Clay Adams enters the kitchen and picks up the phone.

BROTHER JUDE
Clay, it's Bill. Brother Bill. How are you and Josh?

He walks a few steps to the marble table and sits in one of the chairs, facing the pool.

CLAY ADAMS
Bill, great to hear from you. We're good here. How about you?

BROTHER JUDE
Couldn't be better. Say, Josh will be thirty in a week or so.
How are you planning to celebrate?

CLAY ADAMS
I have a big shindig set up for Sunday, October 5th,
and then Josh will work with me full-time at the institute
on the following Monday. He's more than ready to take over.

BROTHER JUDE
The fifth. Great! What time?

CLAY ADAMS
Come to the house around noon. You will be about
an hour early so we can talk.

BROTHER JUDE
Perfect, I will see you then.

40. INT. LIMO—MORNING 40

Clay and Josh ride in the limo.

CLAY ADAMS
We are almost there—I want everyone to meet you
before the party. And I wanted you to meet them
before you work with them on Monday.

The limo stops in front of the institute. They exit and walk to the front door.

CLAY ADAMS (continuing)
You know my secretary's name. Magdalena.

JOSHUA
I have spoken to her on the phone many times. Why?

CLAY ADAMS
That is just it, you have never met her in person,
and I want you to know something about her before you do.

JOSHUA
What's all the mystery? She has been with you for almost
two and a half years, isn't it?

CLAY ADAMS
Yes. There is no real mystery. She has been crippled since birth.
I just never wanted to talk about that with anyone. Not just you.
She has been very good for the institute and me. As you take over the
operations, you don't need to keep her on. I am just saying—

JOSHUA
I am very glad you told me. We don't need to discuss it further now.

The two enter the building.

41. INT. INTERNATIONAL CLONING INSTITUTE MORNING 41

Magdalena (Maggie) approaches the two from a distance, her limp is
very noticeable.

MAGDALENA

Good morning, Mr. Adams. And good morning to the other Mr. Adams about whom I have heard so much. I am very glad to finally meet you.

CLAY ADAMS

Good morning, Magdalena. You are correct. This is my son, Joshua.

Magdalena reaches her hand to shake Joshua's hand. As they shake, Magdalena is instantly healed of her infirmity. She feels something but is not sure what it is. Joshua feels power leave him and looks perplexed.

JOSHUA

Please just call me Josh. I am so happy to finally meet you in person.

Maggie has a quizzical look on her face, confused as to what just happened to her.

MAGDALENA (whispering to herself)
Oh my God!

CLAY ADAMS
Maggie, are you all right?

MAGDALENA

Oh yes, yes, sir. It was just something—I'm okay.
Sir, the board is assembled and waiting for you.

CLAY ADAMS
Yes, we shouldn't keep them waiting.

MAGDALENA
I'm fine. I'll catch up with you later when
I take Joshua on his tour of the facility.

CI AY ADAMS
Very good. Very good. Okay, Josh, let's not keep them waiting.

Clay and Josh walk out of the scene.

Maggie looks down at her leg and shakes her head in dis belief. She begins to walk toward the washroom. She does not limp. She leans on the wall to steady herself. Surprise comes over her as she realizes she is cured. Jorge Longinus, the CFO board member, is walking down the hall to the board meeting. He sees Maggie leaning on the wall with her head down and rushes to her aid. She sees him coming and starts to walk. She fakes a limp so she will not seem any different.

JORGE
Maggie, are you okay?

MAGDALENA
Oh, hi, Jorge, I'm fine—oh, you're late.
They are all waiting for you in the boardroom.

Maggie gets to the washroom and sees that no one else is in the room and then begins to walk normally with no limp, walking in circles and watching herself in the mirror.

MAGDALENA (continuing)
I don't believe this. I can't believe this. I shake hands with him
and...and how? How does this happen. It's a miracle!
It has to be a miracle. Oh my God, thank you!
All these thirty-eight years. Thank you, God. Thank you.

42. INT. BOARDROOM—CONTINUING 42

CLAY ADAMS
And now that you have all met Josh, let me say that he will be
officially coming on board next Monday, the day after his party this
coming Sunday. You all should have received your invitations a month
ago already, and if there was an oversight, please know you are all invited.
And don't bring any gifts. Just bring your presence, yourselves and your
families. And you must have a good time. That's an order.

Clay turns to Josh.

CLAY ADAMS (continuing)
Josh, we will finish this meeting while you go and find Maggie
and take the tour with her.

JOSHUA
It was nice to have met all of you. We will see you at my party.
Bring your families. A man is only thirty once, you know.
Josh leaves the room, and the meeting continues.

CLAY ADAMS
Jorge, would you give us the latest figures, please?

JORGE
Sir, gentlemen, I am happy to finally announce that we
are now the second largest and wealthiest corporation
in the world as of this last month, and we are supplying
the majority market share of cloned beef to every country
in the world except the United States. Many of the countries
take all of their beef from us. As you know, our proprietary process
of cloning is twice as fast as any competitor, and with the US
government now finding that for whatever reason cloned beef is
completely safe and immune from mad cow disease, they will be
placing orders with us in the near future. This should be more than
enough to move us up to being the number one corporation.
The plan then is to double the production of beef within
three months.

43. INT MAGGIE'S OFFICE—CONTINUING 43

Josh peers into the open door to Magdalena's office and sees her sitting
at her desk.

JOSHUA
I guess I am ready for my tour.

MAGDALENA
Great. Then I will ask you to follow me.

Maggie gets up and walks with no limp out of the office and takes Josh down the hallway.

JOSHUA
Please call me Josh.

MAGDALENA
Oh, I will. I will call you anything you wish...
Do you notice anything, Josh?

Josh looks from side to side.

JOSHUA
I am noticing a lot of new things. Did you have
something specific in mind?

They continue to walk through areas of the building.

MAGDALENA
Did your father tell you that I was born crippled?

JOSHUA
Uh... you, you're walking perfectly fine. But you...
you were limping when I met you as I came into
the building earlier this morning?

MAGDALENA
I know! Isn't it wonderful?

JOSHUA
You and Dad are playing a joke on me, aren't you?

MAGDALENA
No. It is all because of you.
Maggie puts her arms around Josh and gives him a
quick kiss on the cheek. Josh is taken aback.

JOSHUA

Me? What does that mean?

MAGDALENA

I don't know how it happened, but when we shook hands, something happened, and that was it. I walked without pain, without shortness of the one leg. What can I tell you? That is what happened.

JOSHUA

I felt something, but I didn't know what to say. I guess we should take the tour, go to lunch, and finish the tour if necessary.

MAGDALENA

Fine. Call me Maggie—please.

44. INT. CLAY ADAM'S OFFICE—LATER 44

Josh appears in the doorway of Clay's office. Clay looks up from his desk.

CLAY ADAMS

There you are. Are you ready to go home and tell me all about your day?

JOSHUA

I certainly am.. .you are not going to believe what happened to Maggie.

Clay gets up from his desk, walks to Josh, and puts his hand on his shoulder.

CLAY ADAMS

Let's go. And tell me all about it. We have a party to get ready for. Sunday will be here before we know it.

45. EXT. PARTY IN BACK OF CLAY'S HOME-AFTERNOON 45

SUPER—Sunday, October 5

Josh looks at his watch, and it is 3:00 PM

JOSHUA (to himself in undertone)
I wonder if she is coming.

Josh walks over to the open-air bar and then glances to one side and sees Magdalena coming around to the back from the front of the house.

MAGDALENA
There's my birthday boy.

She walks right up and kisses him on the lips a bit more quickly this time.

MAGDALENA (continuing)
Happy birthday, Josh. It's great to see you again.
Thanks so much for what you did.

JOSHUA
Let's not talk about it. Can I get you a drink?

Josh takes Maggie by her arm. They walk together to a small refreshment bar where a bartender waits on the guests.

MAGDALENA
Yes, please. Do you have champagne?

JOSHUA (to the bartender)
Two champagnes, please.

Josh takes two flutes of champagne and hands one to Magdalena.

JOSHUA (continuing)
Are you hungry

MAGDALENA
Famished.

JOSHUA
Good.

Josh clinks his flute on hers.

JOSHUA (continuing)
Right over this way, fair lady… I'll catch up
with you after you have eaten.

Maggie looks disappointed. She looks down at her champagne.

MAGDALENA
Okay. Sure. Later...

46.INT.CLAYADAM'SKITCHN/DEN—AFTERNOON 46

CLAY ADAMS
It has been another six months. This has to stop.
You must come over more often. You can get away from
that monastery or chapel or whatever you call it,
if you want. This is the eleventh year of Pope Francis.
(more)

CLAYADAMS (continued)
We have the last Pope in office, Pope Francis, according to
the prophecy we spoke of years ago. How much time do we have?

BROTHER JUDE
I have no idea—I never expected this to go on so long. I am going
to be on my way. I had a great visit with Josh. He is going to be great
with you. This should be the beginning of some big things. He told me
about Maggie. Anyway, please do say goodbye to him for me.

CLAY ADAMS
All right, but for sure you are coming for Thanksgiving
We are having cloned turkey. We will celebrate it, even if no one else in
this country does. Call me in a week—promise?

BROTHER JUDE
Okay. I promise.

Brother Jude gets up to leave the house.

47. EXT. BACKYARD—DUSK 47

Clay closes the glass door of the kitchen/den behind him and approaches the rowdy gang at the party.

CLAY ADAMS
It's time, everyone. We need to sing "Happy Birthday"
and have our cake and eat it too.

Maggie finds Josh and leads him into a group of guests. She waves her arms as if she were conducting an orchestra as she begins to sing. The guests chime in. Before the song ends, Maggie lays a big kiss on Josh's lips.

The guests clap and howl. People finish their cake and drinks and begin to leave. Clay approaches a group of caterers, who are obviously tired after serving so many guests.

CLAY ADAMS (continuing)
You can clean all this up tomorrow.
You don't need to do it now.
Please go home and enjoy your evening.

Clay finds Josh and Maggie, who are holding hands.

CLAY ADAMS (continuing)
I am going to lie down for a little while. Josh, I'll be
up to talk to you before we retire. Uncle Jude did tell
me to say goodbye to you before he left.

JOSHUA
Oh, I wanted to talk to him before he left.
Okay, I will see you in a little bit then.

MAGDALENA
Good night, Mr. Adams. I will be going soon.
I guess I will see you in the morning at work.

CLAY ADAMS
Good night, Maggie. It has been a great day.

Clay leaves them, walks toward the house, and goes inside.

Josh takes Maggie's hand as they walk toward the glowing swimming pool in the dusk.

JOSHUA
You know, this kissing business is going to have to stop.

MAGDALENA
Why? It is just for your birthday.

JOSHUA
We will be working together, you know.

MAGDALENA
Hey, let's go for a swim.

JOSHUA
I wouldn't mind, really. It would be kind of refreshing. Did you bring a suit?

MAGDALENA
Yes, I'll get it. Go get into yours.

Josh goes into the house. Maggie looks around to make sure no one is looking. She takes her blouse off and then her skirt to reveal her seductive bra and panties. She slips slowly into the pool. The full moon is rising in the east as the sun sets.

Josh runs out of the house with a couple of towels. He tosses on a deck chair and dives into the pool. He emerges next to Maggie.

JOSHUA
And you said you had a suit—

MAGDALENA
This is a suit! Anyway, now I can wish you
happy birthday like I wanted to before.

She hangs her arms around his neck and kisses Josh long and passionately.

JOSHUA
I don't think we should be doing this

MAGDALENA
Oh, really?

She puts both hands onto Josh's head and pushes down, dunking him into the water.

MAGDALENA (continuing)
Here is your baptism into the working world,
you captive of your ivory tower.

Lightning flashes from the sky vertically in the distance from where Josh is submerged in the pool. There is no thunder and no rain.

Josh comes out of the water. He demonically grabs her and violently kisses her.

CONTINUED: (3)

At first, she succumbs submissively, but he is too rough. She turns her head to break away. She pushes on his chest and tries to squirm away from him. He is not deterred. He pushes her under the water. She comes up gasping. He tears at her. He will not stop, and it is obvious this is rape.

MAGDALENA (continuing)
What are you doing? Stop. Not this way. You're hurting me!

Josh covers her mouth with his hand. She goes limp and emotionless and lets him finish. When he is spent, Maggie gets out of the pool and grabs a towel and her clothes. She runs to the front of the house where her car is parked. She looks back to Josh, who stands at the pool.

> MAGDALENA (continuing; sobbing in a whisper)
> You fool, you didn't have to rape me—
> I would have been putty in your hands.

Josh turns and walks toward the house.

48. EXT. SECOND STORY WINDOW OF HOUSE CONTINUING 48

Clay looks down at the pool. He does not see Maggie. He looks perturbed. He sees Josh in his wet bathing suit as he approaches the kitchen/den.

> CLAY ADAMS
> What's going on down there?

> JOSHUA
> It's nothing. Everything is fine—go back to bed.

> CLAY ADAMS
> I heard what she said. I'm coming down—

> JOSHUA
> No! Don't—just go to bed.

INT. CLAY'S KITCHEN/DEN

Josh closes the door to the kitchen behind him. He is drip ping water on the slick tiles. He stops. He stands like a zombie staring into space.
Clay enters the kitchen.

CLAY ADAMS
I heard what Maggie said. Don't tell me I didn't hear right.
Stop staring into space—look at me. Talk!
Josh comes out of the zombie state. He turns slowly towards Clay.

JOSHUA
No. You talk to me. You tell me about my mother.
I'm not ready for this life you are pushing me into.
I'm not ready for life at all. I've learned all kinds of things,
but I don't know anything about people...I don't know anything.

CLAY ADAMS
Just calm down.

Clay walks further into the kitchen. Josh backs away. Clay pushes forward.

CLAY ADAMS (continuing)
Josh, you weren't adopted. I made you, you weren't an adopted—

JOSHUA
What? What did you say?

CLAY ADAMS
I didn't mean that—I mean I didn't mean to say that—

JOSHUA
But you did say it, and now you are going to tell me everything.
Everything. You get it—you don't have a choice now.

CLAY ADAMS
All right, the truth is...the truth is you were cloned.

JOSHUA
You cloned me? What do you mean?
What can that possibly mean? That is illegal.
That is just another one of your escape answers—

CLAY ADAMS

No, it is true, and it is just as well you finally know
the truth anyway. I don't know how I got into this in the first
place—it was your Uncle Billy's doing—

JOSHUA

Oh! Blame it on Uncle Billy again.

CLAY ADAMS

I guess you can say that I am your mother and
father because I cloned you for Uncle Billy.

JOSHUA

Here comes the double talk again...
you cloned me for Uncle Billy.

CLAY ADAMS

We can talk this through, Josh.
We'll go over everything in time.

JOSHUA

No, not in time but right now. You make such a point to
never lie to me, and you tell me there is no Santa Claus because
you don't want to lie to me, and now you tell me I am a clone!
Holy cow, no, we won't talk about it! You are not my father,
and you are not my mother—I don't even look like you.

Clay comes toward Josh, and Josh backs out of the pool of water to get
away from him. Clay reaches out for Josh.

JOSHUA (continuing)

Get away from me.

Josh pushes the old man. Clay slips into the water. He falls. His head
hits the countertop, and then his body lands with a sickening thud. He does
not move.

Josh stands with his back to the old man for several seconds.

JOSHUA (continuing)
Okay, cut out the bullshit. Get up. I said get up!
Josh goes to the body and feels for a pulse. There is none.

JOSHUA (continuing)
Oh my God, what else can go wrong?

Josh reverts to his zombie-like state. He walks stiffly like a robot to the wall phone and dials 911. Josh looks down at Clay. Clay's eyes are open and unfocused.

JOSHUA (continuing)
I have an emergency. It's all my fault. My father slipped on water I tracked him into the kitchen, and I think he's dead. It's my fault. I tracked the water in. Please get here fast—he's not breathing—I can't find a pulse—what can I do?

OPERATOR (OS)
We're on the way. Go to the front door and make sure it is open.

50. EXT. FRONT OF CLAY'S HOUSE—CONTINUING 50

The door opens slowly. Josh stands in the doorway. A siren wails in the distance.

JOSHUA
Now I have to lie to cover this up.

51. EXT. CEMETERY CATHOLIC FUNERAL—DAY 51

The funeral is over, and everyone is leaving and driving away. Maggie walks to her car but does not get in. She stands by the passenger door. Brother Jude and Josh are the only two left at the grave site.

BROTHER JUDE
Josh, I will be leaving the order.

Josh, who has been standing in a zombie-like state, turns quickly toward Brother Jude (soon to become known as Uncle Billy).

BROTHER JUDE (continuing)
I will move in with you. We'll be good companions together. I should never have become a cleric— it was a mistake from the beginning.

JOSHUA
You don't have to do anything for me. I will be all right...Uncle Billy.

UNCLE BILLY
I'm doing it for myself. I never should have entered the order. I am the executor of your dad's estate, and you will need help now that you will be one of the richest men in the world, if not the richest.

JOSHUA
First of all, your brother was not my dad, and I will talk to you about that later, not now.

UNCLE BILLY
What! How do you know that?

JOSHUA
Clay told me with his dying breath—or should I say with his lying breath. Now go. Your car is waiting.

UNCLE BILLY
Can't I give you a ride?
Josh looks to see Maggie waiting at her car near Uncle Billy's limo. All the other cars are gone.

JOSHUA
I have a ride. We will talk to you later.

Josh stays at the grave. Brother Jude walks to his limo. As Brother Jude's car pulls away, Josh walks directly toward Maggie. As he gets closer and closer, she leans back against the auto. When Josh gets to her, he falls to his knees, grabs her hips, and puts his cheek against her stomach. She looks down on him lovingly.

JOSHUA (continuing)
I don't have a father or a mother, Maggie.

MAGDALENA
I know, but...

JOSHUA
No. You don't know.

He looks up into her eyes.

JOSHUA (continuing)
I was cloned. I never knew it until now.

MAGDALENA
What? Don't be silly—it doesn't matter, I love you.

JOSHUA
How can you? I am such a fool.

MAGDALENA
No, you're not, and I am sorry I called you that.
I didn't understand at all, but I love you, and I will always love you.

JOSHUA
Really?

Maggie pulls Josh's arms to raise him to his feet, and she puts his arms around her neck. They kiss passionately.

MAGDALENA
Take me home and make love to me.

52. EXT. CLAY'S HOME—SUNRISE 52

A taxi stops. Josh gets out of the taxi. Uncle Billy opens the front door.

UNCLE BILLY
Where have you been?

Uncle Billy looks at Josh. Josh is rumpled—he needs a shave, and his hair is matted.

UNCLE BILLY (continuing)
Never mind, come in.

53. INT. CLAY ADAMS HOME—CONTINUING 53

JOSHUA
Maggie said the institute can take care of itself for a while and not to worry.

UNCLE BILLY
I just made coffee.

54. INT. KITCHEN/DEN—CONTINUING 54

Clay and Josh sit at the kitchen table. Clay finishes pouring coffee into Josh's cup and moves on to fill his cup.

JOSHUA
So now I'm listening. You didn't disagree with me
at the cemetery when I told you I was cloned.
So you know, don't you?

UNCLE BILLY
It is more my fault than anyone else's. Did your
father—I mean, did Clay tell you how you were cloned?

JOSHUA
There wasn't time.

UNCLE BILLY
Okay, I'll tell you the whole story. The illusion
of time passing to midday.

JOSHUA
I don't believe it. I mean I do believe it,
but I cannot believe you would think that you
could get away with something like that.

UNCLE BILLY
We didn't even know if it would work, but it did.
Look at you, you're a powerhouse. You just have to let
the power take over...I hoped you could be the one to
bring peace to the world. And maybe even God would use
your body for His second coming. I didn't have it all throughout,
that's true and that's bad, but when I saw the sparrows in the backyard—

JOSHUA
I never did anything like that again or anything like it. At least, until...

UNCLE BILLY
Until what? Until when?

JOSHUA
Until Maggie.

UNCLE BILLY
Maggie? I don't understand.

JOSHUA
She was born a cripple.

UNCLE BILLY
Yeah, I remember Clay mentioning that once or twice. So?

JOSHUA
So a few days ago, when I met her, we shook hands.

UNCLE BILLY
And?

JOSHUA
And she was completely healed when I touched her...
according to her. That never happened to me
before either as far as I know.

UNCLE BILLY
You mean instantly?

JOSHUA
Yes.

UNCLE BILLY
See—that's exactly what I'm talking about—
that's what the world needs right now.

JOSHUA
Right now, it's pretty scary to me.

UNCLE BILLY
Get over it. You have a responsibility and I'd like to
see you as president of the European Union.

JOSHUA
Yeah, well...maybe I'd like to see you become the Pope...
and just how do you think that is going to happen?

UNCLE BILLY
The good that needs to be done can best be done in a
position like that. The history of man is a history of war—it
pains me to even think about what people do to each
other every second of the day. Every hour of every day,
Josh and you can make the difference. I know it.
One day at a time. Trust me.

JOSHUA
I want to be a man of peace. I'll do whatever I can.
I have some ideas for the institute, and we will have the
resources to carry out the plan. I told Maggie that I would be
at the institute on October thirty-first for the board meeting,
but I will call her tomorrow to arrange for a special board
meeting for next Monday so I can get started as early as possible.

UNCLE BILLY
I will be with you all the way, Josh.

55. INT. BOARDROOM OF THE INSTITUTE —MORNING 55

Josh, with complete confidence, getting stronger every day and leading
to arrogance, marches to the head of a large polished wood conference table.
He sits down. Board members are seated at their places in high back soft
leather chairs. They look to him.

JOSHUA
Thank you all for coming to this special meeting called at the
last minute. As you know, the sudden, tragic, and accidental death of
my father puts me in charge, and so I will be nominated and elected as
chairman of the board. Let's get the nomination approved and passed
immediately.

BOARD MEMBER 1 (obsequiously)
I nominate Joshua Adams as the new chairman of the board
and CEO of the International Cloning Institute.

Board Member 2 stands to emphasize the moment.

JORGE
I second that motion.

Jorge sits down with an officious smile.

JOSHUA
Thank you, Jorge. Mr. CFO?

SECRETARY
All in favor, signify by saying aye.

Everyone votes yes.

SECRETARY (continuing)
Any opposed, signify by saying nay.

Silence. No one votes no. All the board members are looking up to Josh—except Jorge.

SECRETARY (continuing)
It is unanimous then. Mr. Joshua C. Adams is hereby elected the new Chairman of the Board of Directors and CEO of I.C.I.

JOSHUA
Jorge, I want you to raise the price of our beef
by ten cents a pound immediately.

JORGE
Uh, okay...

JOSHUA
And if anyone objects, cut off their shipments for fourteen days.

JORGE
Yes, sir...very good.

JOSHUA
Cut all shareholder dividends and begin the accumulation
of a cash position. Make a donation designated in
US dollars of one billion to the European Union by wire transfer.
Lastly, for now, as soon as I leave this meeting, move and
pass a resolution to have board meetings every year rather
than the current once-a-month stipulation.

Josh stands.

JOSHUA (continuing)
I bid you good day, gentlemen. See you next year.

56. INT. OUTSIDEI.C.I. BOARDROOM—CONTINUING 56

Josh exits the boardroom. The door closes behind him. Maggie is sitting at her desk in the posh offices.

JOSHUA
Maggie makes a three-o'clock appointment for tomorrow with the President of the European Union—at his office.

MAGDALENA
Very good, sir.

She rises and leaves the room to execute the directive.

57. INT. OFFICES OF THE EUROPEAN UNION

The receptionist sees Mr. Joshua Adams coming into the office and rises before he can even get to her and walks around her desk.

RECEPTIONIST
Mr. Adams, we have been expecting you.
Right this way. Mr. Hammarskjold is expecting you.

With deference, the receptionist takes Josh to the office of Bjorn Hammarskjold.

JOSHUA
Good afternoon, sir.
Josh extends his right hand to shake with Hammarskjold, and Hammarskjold meets it with his left hand. Josh sees Hammarskjold's right remain stiffly at his side.

JOSHUA (continuing)
No, please, your right hand.

Hammarskjold reluctantly reaches his right hand as far as possible, and Josh takes it. The crippled hand is immediately healed and is normal in every way. The man is dumbfounded.

He slumps into his chair in an almost hypnotic state. Josh takes a seat.

JOSHUA (continuing)
You did receive the donation?

The man shakes his head yes hypnotically.

BJORN HAMMARSKJOLD
Yes, it was greatly appreciated.
Now we have the resources to continue our—

JOSHUA
I need you to resign as head of this august body in
order for me to replace you—as soon as possible.

BJORN HAMMARSKJOLD
Certainly, the board meets on Friday, and I will see to it...
we will schedule the swearing-in—what day is good for you?

JOSHUA
October thirty-first. I'll be in touch.

Josh imediately gets up and walks out of the office, leaving Hammarskjold looking at his right hand. He picks up a pencil and stares at his fingers.

58. EXT. SWEARING IN CEREMONY—DAY 58

Josh is at a podium above about five hundred people who listen in silence. The audience does not move but stands rigid as if at attention. Autumn leaves rustle and fall from trees splattered with colors of yellow and red.

As Josh speaks, the camera pulls farther and farther away.

The camera comes behind an assassin preparing a .50-caliber rifle with scope. He is a mile away in the hills surrounding the ceremonial area. In camouflage, he blends in perfectly with the fallen leaves. Slowly, the camera reveals that the assassin is Jorge Longinus, the CFO. We barely hear Bjorn Hammarskjold's voice as he introduces Josh as the new president. He is interrupted by the much louder cheering of the crowd.

JORGE (whispering out loud)
Unbelievable. Arrogant piece of shit, suspending dividends,
who from hell does this guy think he is anyway?
He's just skin and bones, they'll see—
Josh replaces Hammarskjold at the podium.

JOSHUA
Ladies and gentlemen, dignitaries from all federated countries,
I graciously greet you as the President of the European Union,
having been duly sworn in by your former director and dear friend,
Bjorn Hammarskjold. I am sure you are all surprised at
the speed at which all this has taken place, but it was necessary,
I assure you. The peace of this world hangs in the balance,
and peace is of the utmost concern to all responsible people throughout
the world. The first step necessary to win peace is to defeat hunger.
(more)

JOSHUA (continued)
Therefore, my company, the International Cloning Institute,
will be known as the World Cloning Institute, and henceforth from
this day forward, the World Cloning Institute will supply cloned
beef to all peaceful nations of our earth at extremely reasonable prices,
which will be reduced as time passes and our programs meet their targets.
The crowd cheers and cheers. It does not subside but becomes louder
and louder. Josh raises his arms to calm the crowd. The cheering stops.

JOSHUA (continuing)
If a nation or any group of nations turns from peace to
become an aggressor to subjugate other countries,

their ration of cloned beef will be suspended to be resumed
only on my approval and after meeting my criteria.

We hear the rifle's report. The bullet strikes the side of Joshua's forehead. He goes down. There is pandemonium, but the gunman is so far away no one has a chance to know where it came from.

Security men cordon off the fallen Josh. Hammarskjold takes Josh's pulse on his neck. There is none. A security guard rushes with a tablecloth, and they place it over his head and torso.

A medical team arrives. Hammarskjold makes way for the doctor. The doctor pulls back the sheet. The doctor checks the vitals and shakes his head and replaces the tablecloth. Josh's blood forms two sixes, and a third six starts to bleed through the cloth.

Hammarskjold returns to the podium.

BJORN HAMMARSKJOLD
Ladies and gentlemen, there does not appear to
be any further danger to any of us, so we can just...

58. CONTINUED: 58

On the clear day, nevertheless, there is a flash of vertical lightning and no thunder as in the swimming pool rape scene.

Josh sits up with the cloth on his head. Hammarskjold turns to look. His mouth falls open. The audience gasps. Josh pulls the sheet off abruptly. Hammarskjold staggers aside. Josh takes the podium.

JOSHUA
It will take more than a bullet to stop our march to peace.
Aggression will not win. Never! What I have said,
I have said and will not change.

Josh exits quickly. Everyone is stunned and speechless. Not a sound is heard except for the rustling of leaves and the heavy door of a limousine shutting after Josh climbs in, holding a bloody hand to his wound. The limousine speeds away through empty streets. An exuberant roar from the stadium breaks the silence.

59. EXT. WORLD CLONING INSTITUTE—NEXT DAY 59

Uncle Billy anxiously waits for Josh on the steps of the institute. Josh's limousine pulls into view. Uncle Billy walks quickly to meet the car before it stops. Billy is at the side door as it stops. He opens the door for Josh. Josh looks up at him to reveal that he has no serious injury to his head. Josh is completely healed with only a mark on his forehead.

UNCLE BILLY
Josh, you can't come in here like that!

Uncle Billy motions to Josh to slide over to make room for him.

JOSHUA
What?

Uncle Billy gets into the car.

60. INT. LIMOUSINE—CONTINUING 60

Uncle Billy pulls a white cap out of his breast pocket.

UNCLE BILLY
Put this on.

JOSHUA
Oh, I understand.

UNCLE BILLY
You've got to blend in a little...listen, something strange is happening.

JOSHUA
More assassins?

UNCLE BILLY
No, but there is an increase in stillborn deaths—can
you guess how many people were born yesterday when
you were shot and how many stillborns there were?

JOSHUA
Please—just tell me. How am I supposed to know that?

UNCLE BILLY
A hundred and forty-four thousand were born! The stinger
is another hundred thousand plus were born dead, I mean stillborn...

JOSHUA
What does this mean? Let's talk further later
at the house after work.

UNCLE BILLY
I'll see you then.

61. EXT. ENTRANCE TO W.C.I.—CONTINUING 61

Uncle Billy gets out of the limousine and holds the door open for Josh. Josh gets out wearing the white cap. Uncle Billy gets back into the limo and drives off in the back of the limousine.

62. INT. JOSH'S OFFICE—CONTINUING 62

Josh is standing, looking out the window of his office. The door opens behind him, but we do not know who has entered.

JORGE
Sir? You wanted to talk to me?

Josh slowly turns from the window to look at Jorge. Jorge is staring, and his mouth drops as Josh takes off the white cap and throws it at Jorge. Jorge backs away as Josh walks slowly toward him.

JOSHUA
Surprise!

Jorge is backed into the door. Josh puts his hand on Jorge's shoulder. Jorge seems to sink with the weight.

JOSHUA (continuing)
Let's just say that I know what you did. From now on,
you will do as I say. Understand?

JORGE
I understand, sir.

JOSHUA
You will triple my salary and give yourself a fifty-percent raise.
Now go. Do not tell anyone of this conversation.

JORGE
Yes, sir.
Josh releases his captive. Jorge slithers out the door.
Josh puts the cap back on his head.

FADE OUT: 63. INT. UNCLE BILLY'S HOME (FORMERLY CLAY ADAMS' HOUSE)—DAY 63

FADE IN:

SUPER—Fifty Days Later

Uncle Billy is sitting at the kitchen table, scribbling notes. The big screen television is tuned to a news channel just loud enough to hear. Josh walks in.

JOSHUA
What's the latest?

UNCLE BILLY
So far… the tally for forty consecutive days was exactly only
one hundred forty-four thousand births each day with
the death rate remaining normal. However, in the last ten days,
no one has been born, but no one has died either.

JOSHUA
Whoa—are you sure?

UNCLE BILLY
Reports as of today say that one thousand births
occurred along with, apparently, exactly one thousand deaths.

JOSHUA
I had Maggie check the total world population today— as you
suspected—6.66 billion—and not changing.

UNCLE BILLY
That's it—this means that we are all here.

JOSHUA
Yes. All here for judgment. We are in living bodies now
to be judged. This is going to cause horror at best
and panic at worst…someone dies and immediately
he is born back again… and humanity…

Uncle Billy finishes the thought.

UNCLE BILLY
Is at the end of six thousand years since Adam and Eve…
the Bible records that Adam was created on the sixth day.
"Breaking News" flashes across the television screen,
interrupting Josh. Both men stop to watch and hear
the television anchor announce.

BROADCAST ANCHOR
The Earth may get another Sun within a week. Light from
Betelgeuse, the Red Giant Star on the right shoulder of Orion,
has just reached the Earth after traveling over three hundred
light years. The light shows the star exploding as a supernova.
Astronomers theorize that if enough radiation hits the gasses
of Jupiter, they will ignite to make a second sun in our
solar system. There will be more later, but for now, everyone is

advised to stay indoors for at least thirty days at that time of the
day when the star is overhead in your locale. More information
as to when the star is overhead will be announced as soon
as we receive the official calculation—stay tuned.

JOSHUA

It is the end of the sixth one-thousand- year day since it all began...

UNCLE BILLY

It seems we have reached the end of exactly the two-thousandth-year
anniversary of the death of our Savior, Jesus Christ.

JOSHUA

Two days...so this is the morning of the third day when Jesus is
resurrected...

UNCLE BILLY

It says in Genesis, "Let us make man in our image, in our likeness."
Josh looks out the window in a state of deep concentration.

JOSHUA

The Bible also says that Yahshua—Jesus—is the expressed image of God.
God made Adam, the son of God, the first man. But he sinned.
(more)

JOSHUA (continued)

So God made Jesus, the last Adam. Jesus is like a mold so that we can be
made like Him by receiving His Holy Spirit to indwell us—

UNCLE BILLY

I get it—the spirit of Jesus is replicated, the Holy Spirit we need
to ask into our heart so that we may be born again... just like
it entered into the Apostles fifty days after Jesus rose from
the dead and ascended to the right hand of God.

JOSHUA

That's why Jesus couldn't send the Holy Spirit until after

returning to the Father so his Spirit could be duplicated—a
kind of spiritual cloning.

UNCLE BILLY
How long would you expect this equal death and birth
thing to continue? Any thoughts?

JOSHUA
God only knows. 'Til the end, I guess.

FADE OUT:

64. EXT. DOME OF THE ROCK—DAY 64

SUPER—Thursday, April 10, 2027—Passover

In the background, the mosque is in the sun. In the foreground, there
is a podium, and a man dressed as a rabbi begins to speak to a large outdoor
audience.

LEVI WEIZMANN
Good afternoon. I am Levi Weizmann, and I will talk later.
Right now, I have the honor of introducing the next three speakers.
But before I do that, there are two events worth noting.
(more)

LEVI WEIZMANN (continued)
One is that there is a red heifer that was born in Bethlehem
three days ago, and two, the diligent interfaith expeditions
searching for the Ark of the Covenant in Ethiopia are on
the verge of an important breakthrough.

The crowd applauds.

LEVI WEIZMANN (continuing)
And now for our first speaker on this important
day for all religions, His Holiness Pope Francis will talk about
relocating the Vatican to Jerusalem. Next, Joshua Adams,
the man who spearheaded this miraculous agreement, will speak

on the importance of our three major religions sharing this holy site. Lastly, we will hear from Mohammed bin Pahlavi, speaking for the Islamic Mecca leadership. Then I will return to say a few words about our Jewish faithful having use of one-third of the Temple on the Mount. So, to begin, I am honored to introduce to you Pope Francis.

Weizmann relinquishes the podium to the Pope, who is dressed for the occasion in red and white robes.

POPE FRANCIS

Greetings to all here and to all the faithful of our three major religions around the globe. As you have just heard, the seat of the Holy Roman Catholic Church will move from Rome to Jerusalem as soon as possible with God's help. Today is a momentous day in the history of our three religions, and it has taken the cooperation of us all to achieve the sharing of this most holy of places.
(more)

POPE FRANCIS (continued)

You heard that expeditions continue to search for the Ark of the Covenant. It is our wish and hope that these expeditions will continue and be fruitful—and to that end, we support these efforts completely. Today, I want to speak about the items that will be found inside the Ark, when it is found. First, there are the stone tablets of the Ten Commandments as carved by the finger of God. This will emphasize the importance of law and grace. Grace and law as coequals in the attainment of eternal life. Second, there is manna, signifying that God always provides. And lastly, there will be found the rod of Aaron that budded when the staffs of competitors were impotent. This showed that Aaron was chosen by God to be the priest for the people. Later, the people demanded their selection of one king after another. This brought destruction, death, and captivity as slaves.

POPE FRANCIS (continuing)

The blind to lead the blind. In closing, I bless you all, in nominee patre... The Pope leaves the podium, and Weizmann takes his place.

LEVI WEIZMANN
Thank you, Pope Francis. Our next speaker is Joshua Adams, the man who knew that all this was possible as well as necessary for our religions.

JOSHUA
Thank you, Rabbi Weizmann, and thank you, Your Eminence, and thank you, Mohammed and ladies and gentlemen. I never think that anything is impossible. Miracles happen.
(more)

JOSHUA (continued)
Miracles happen every day. I have persuaded the three major religions to share this religious site instead of fighting to control all of it by one of them.

As God's representative on earth, I persuaded them to realize that the Arab world will worship in this holy place on Thursday night and Friday. The Jewish world will worship on Friday night and Saturday Sabbath, and our Christian brothers will have Saturday night and Sunday. I can always lead, and people will follow. They will follow my directive to work rapidly for peace and harmony. I am to be honored and worshipped in that regard. The camera pans the crowd and comes to rest on Cardinal DeVille, who is standing next to his friend and former clergyman, Uncle Billy. The cardinal turns to whisper to his friend.

CARDINAL DEVILLE
No offense, Bill, but this reminds me of the abomination of desolation… the Antichrist standing in the Holy Place as written in the Book of Daniel. Uncle Billy frowns and nods in agreement.

UNCLE BILLY
I'm afraid so.

Lightning flashes, stunning everyone. The real Jesus appears in the cloudless sky. Ghostlike and resembling an aged Josh with white hair, we see He is followed by winged angels in the millions. Select people in the crowd begin to levitate and are raptured. Their faces glow and smile, and their arms are raised to Jesus. We see Brother Adrian floating up from the earth and joining the spirits.

People on earth panic. They run and hide as if the sky were falling, but others watch—watch as people are raised to follow Jesus to the heavens.

We see Jesus close up: His hair is white as wool, his eyes like flames of fire, gird with a gold belt, and he says, "I am that I am," and his tongue becomes a two-edged sword as it comes out of his mouth and all the way down to cut off the head of Josh Adams at the podium. Jesus and all the angels and the chosen to recede into the distance with their Savior.

People in the crowd seem relieved. We see Cardinal DeVille and Uncle Billy standing where they were earlier.

CARDINAL DEVILLE
This is the rapture—and we are not chosen?

UNCLE BILLY
Does this mean Josh is the AntiChrist?

CARDINAL DEVILLE
I'm afraid so.

DISSOLVE TO:

65. INT. UNCLE BILLY'S KITCHEN—DAY 65

The television is on, and the same anchor is speaking. Jack, Cardinal DeVille, is out of his vestments and sits at the table. Uncle Billy enters the kitchen.

SUPER—Seven Days Later

CARDINAL DEVILLE
It's been a hell of a week, Bill—

UNCLE BILLY
In more ways than one...How does it feel to be out
of those vestments, Jack?

CARDINAL DEVILLE
A lot better, especially since they just reported that in every country,

places of worship of all religions are being burned—apparently by people who thought they were going to be raptured but weren't. Cardinal DeVille points to the television. Uncle Billy sits at the table.

65. CONTINUED: 65

CARDINAL DEVILLE (continuing)
Listen...

BROADCAST ANCHOR
The river Euphrates has been dammed in Turkey, apparently preparing the way for some two hundred million terrorists from every country to cross it and destroy Jerusalem. How former enemies have become allies in terrorism is beyond understanding. We take you to Suzanne Newcastle,our correspondent in Jerusalem.

A woman, Suzanne Newcastle, speaks from an insert in the TV screen.

SUZANNE NEWCASTLE
The first wave of terrorists has reached the old city.
You can hear the gunfire.

The camera appears to go into the television, transporting us to Jerusalem.

66. EXT.JERUSALEM—CONTINUING 66

A flash of light is seen again as Jesus and all the angels and saints appear in the heavens. Hailstones of fifty pounds fall on the terrorists. Also, other terrorists are seen to have their flesh and eyes melt in the sockets before their bodies hit the ground. The camera shows all the same things happening in every culture in every country around the world.

67. EXT. ST.PETER'S SQUARE—CONTINUING 67

The Pope is standing on the balcony. He is trying to calm the masses that have rushed into the square as the ice boulders fall on Rome. A boulder hits the square, killing many.

Another hits the balcony and takes out the Pope and the people who stood with him.

68. INT. UNCLE BILLY'S KITCHEN—CONTINUING 68

Uncle Billy and Cardinal DeVille are where we last saw them.
A huge hailstone crashes into the swimming pool. Another stone hits the window with a crash.
The television blanks out. A stone crashes into the ceiling above the two friends. The scene cuts to black.

DISSOLVE TO:

69. EXT. WORLD CLONING INSTITUTE/I.C.I BUILDING—DAY 69

The building is in ruins. Boulders arc resting on pulverized walls. Two men are standing in the foreground. They are in a daze.

SURVIVOR #1
I guess we're left behind. I always wondered what they were doing in this place.

SURVIVOR #2
What are we supposed to do now?

SURVIVOR #1
You mean after we clean up this mess?

SURVIVOR #2
Yeah! I mean what are we supposed to do—we are not unholy but we are not holy enough either...

SURVIVOR #1
There was a guy that I saw in the Rapture seven days ago—everyone thought he was crazy because he taught that Saturday was the Sabbath and that there would be a second Rapture seven years from the first.

SURVIVOR #2
You mean he said a second Rapture?

SURVIVOR #1
I remember he said that the figure of one hundred forty-four thousand is mentioned twice in the Book of Revelation. Everyone assumes it is the same group—

SURVIVOR #2
You mean there is still hope—

SURVIVOR #1
Not unless you are Jewish.

SURVIVOR #2
What do you mean?

SURVIVOR #1
The guy taught that the first group were Christian believers, which could include Jewish messianic believers, but the second group of one hundred forty-four thousand is specifically designated as twelve thousand from each tribe.

SURVIVOR #2
What is the purpose of that?

SURVIVOR #1
Well, sometime after the second Rapture, whether it is seven more years or whatever, they all come back to be teachers for a thousand years in resurrection bodies that cannot be killed.

SURVIVOR #2
Yeah, it will probably take me, at least, that long to learn all this stuff anyway—

SURVIVOR #1
At least, it would seem like eternal life if we lived a thousand years with no assholes on the planet.

SURVIVOR #2
Yeah... I'm Jewish.

FADE OUT:

We hear "What if God Was One of Us" by Joan Osborne as credits roll over black. After about thirty seconds of the song that continues, the credits stop rolling on black.

FADE IN:

News footage as if on television of an anchor at his desk.

BROADCAST ANCHOR
This just in from CERN in Switzerland—the Hadron Particle Accelerator has reported that the God Particle has been found after a collision in the cloud chamber... and we have footage from CERN of the cloud chamber.

CUT TO:

The mist of a cloud starts to clear. The face of Jesus is seen as it was on the shroud as seen in the opening.

SUPER—Just kidding!

The super dissolves out.

SUPER—But then again...

The super dissolves out while the credits roll. The song we heard in the opening, "What if God Was One of Us," continues until it is finished.

FADE OUT:

AFTERWORD

The author has a personal speculative opinion. This means it is not necessarily a fact.

The author believes that Jesus may have been a clone of Adam, the first man, who was the son of God as stated in the book of Luke.

Mary's words to the angel were, "Be it done unto me according to your word." The author's belief does qualify as a possibility of being the "it." The cell would have been taken from Adam at the time Eve was created. This was before original sin.

Some additional observations that make this idea plausible are the words in Genesis, "The seed of the woman shall crush his head." A woman does not have "seed" but an egg.

Also, the most used title for Jesus is "Son of Man." According to the facts of Jesus's existence, this would be the last thing to call Him. In fact, "son of woman" would be more on point. But if the son of man should be translated as "Son of Adam," it is more understandable. Jesus is called the last Adam in Scripture.

If Jesus were a clone of Adam, He would have no DNA from Mary. Thus, she would not have had to be born immaculately, without original sin as taught by Rome. This is a doctrine for which there is little or no scriptural support in any way.

The author has seen only one recent presentation of a DNA analysis of the blood on the shroud, and it was not Jewish. It was called Druze, which predates Jewish DNA. The author has seen no confirmation of this presentation.

Just some thoughts for your consideration.

STATEMENT OF BELIEFS YAHWEH'S CHILDREN OF OBEDIENCE

We believe that our members will be distinguished in:

1. their love for Yahweh with all their being; and
2. the equality of their love for themselves and others.

Yahweh is the name of the Most High Triune God, and Yahshua (Jesus) is one of the three.

We believe that as new historical and archaeological facts come to light and the Holy Spirit further enlightens our understanding of Scripture, we will be "guided into all truth," not just some (John 16:13).

We firmly believe that when Yahshua comes for His bride (His body), only the churches holding to the beliefs as set forth below will be able to come close to saying, "Yes, Yahshua, You will find the faith on earth when You come" (Luke 10:8).

We believe that humans, as created by God, are composed of two things—matter and spirit—which when combined form a third thing, a living soul, a human being (Genesis 2:7; Zechariah 12:1).

When the two parts are separated, as we read in James 2:26, "The body without the spirit is dead." The result is that the human spirit (breath of God) returns to God from whence it came, and the body returns to the earth" (Ecclesiastes 12:7).

Thus, there is no soul when the body and spirit are separated.

Remember Yahshua's last words, "Into your hands, I commit my *spirit*" not my *soul* (Luke 23:46).

There is no more living human being as long as the body and spirit are separated, but the soul is *restored* at the resurrection of the body when the same spirit is reunited with the same body by Yahweh (Psalm 23:3)

Part of our being is earthly, a created substance, and the other part, the breath of God, is from God, never said to be created.

We believe that the analogy of a water molecule helps us to understand this situation. When the hydrogen and oxygen are combined, there exists a water molecule. When we take the two elements apart, both still exist, but a water molecule no longer exists. The body and the spirit of a person still exist in some form after death, but the "living soul" *is no more* until resurrected. The Bible refers to this as sleeping in several places.

We believe that every person who does not "die in Christ" with the Holy Spirit joined with his or her human spirit goes to hell, a holding stat until the resurrection to either eternal life or the second death, never to exist again (Ecclesiastes 9:5; Revelation 21:18). If a person dies without the Holy Spirit in their heart as a new creation, they might as well not have been born.

Our only hope for eternal life is to be resurrected by the one *who told us he is the resurrection and the life*, as He did when He raised Lazarus from the dead (John 11:25).

We believe that humans, when born, because of "the fall," are only *creatures* of God but not *children* of God until fertilized by the Holy Spirit when we become adopted by our Creator (Romans 8:1 5).

Fortunately, the Bible tells us that we can be given the "power" to become children of God (John 1:12). We need to repent, ask for forgiveness, and be baptized by total immersion at age twenty or more and then receive the laying on of hands by a person who has the indwelling Holy Spirit and who can confer Him upon us (Hebrews 6:1—6).

We believe in infant baptism but only in anticipation of the future day when the child, now an adult, voluntarily accepts Yahshua as his or her Messiah, Lord, and Master.

We believe that the statement in Genesis where Yahweh says, "Let us make man in our image, in our likeness," is a two-step process.

1. Yahshua is the expressed image of Yahweh (Hebrews 1:3).
2. To make the likeness of Yahshua's image in us is only accomplished when we receive the Holy Spirit as if it were Yahshua's Spirit being cloned and then given to us humans, making us a "new creation" and able to say, "When you see Me (now a capital M), you see Yahshua."

The creation of Adam was to make an image of God, but Adam "fell." Since the fall, we are all children of Adam, not of God. If we were all children of God when born, we would not need the "power to become children of God" (John 1:12).

So any humans born outside the Garden of Eden, in Adam's lineage, are sons of Adam and disowned by God. Adam is a type of Satan. Adam was created perfect, but he fell, choosing to transgress God's Laws (1 John 3:4). By committing the original sin, Adam, with all his descendants, was condemned to the death penalty, born to die—"The wages of sin is death."

We believe that after the Holy Spirit has been joined with a human spirit, together they become a "new creation." The human is only then able to keep the Laws of God. Before a human is conceived again, their attempt to keep the Laws of God is no more meaningful than a man sitting on death row keeping the laws and thereby claiming that his death sentence should not be imposed. He is "already condemned" for his previous crime (John 3:18).

Yes, you and I have sinned before coming to planet Earth for which we are "already condemned." We do not need to know what the sins are, but we should know that we have sinned. This realization makes the scripture, "All have sinned...," understandable since all include a one-second-old baby (Romans 3:23).

Our process of reconciliation to Yahweh is:

1.To be born of Adam. There is no forgiveness of sin without the shedding of blood (Hebrews 9:22). "Straight is the gate and narrow is the way that leads to life (the birth canals of our mothers) and few find it" (Matthew 7:14). We are now multiplying and filling the earth as originally commanded in Genesis. So today there are many more people on earth than there were when this scripture was given.
2.To be conceived again from above by receiving the Holy Spirit, which becomes one with our human spirit. Only then are we a "new creation" to ultimately be "born again" at the resurrection from the dead (Romans 8:16)?

We believe that a person can only commit the unpardonable sin of blasphemy against the Holy Spirit if he or she has already received Him into their heart (spirit) and then rejected Him. It is as if "they have put their hand to the plow and looked back" (Luke 9:62). They have "tasted of the heavenly gift" and deemed Him to be undesirable (Hebrews 6:4).

As a "new creation," what Laws are believers supposed to obey? What Laws are to be written on the two tablets of our hearts as a "new creation"? The minimum starting point is the Ten Commandments, not nine! We believe that we are com manded not to take the name of Yahweh in vain (Exodus 20). But the sacred names should often be used in praise. Hallelujah! Yahweh!

To be empowered to obey the Ten Commandments, besides needing the power of the Holy Spirit, one needs to know when the Sabbath Day begins and when it ends, and when a new month begins to know when the annual Sabbath days are to be celebrated (Leviticus 23).

We believe the weekly Sabbath Day begins Saturday morning at first light before sunrise and ends Sunday morning at first light (see pamphlet When Do Days Begin). Every creation day, God did things before "there was evening and morning" (a night of rest).

We believe the new moon begins at the conjunction of the sun and moon. We walk by faith, not by (eye)sight or sighting a sliver of a crescent moon. King David, as every shepherd knows, discovered that after two nights of seeing no moon, the conjunction must have taken place, starting the first day of a new month the next morning of the third day. Thus, he could say, "Tomorrow is the new moon" (1 Samuel 20:5 and 18). (See pamphlet describing how Yahshua and the apostles celebrated the Passover Last Supper one night before the nation of Israel celebrated their Jewish Passover because they started their month one day late.)

This does not negate the Sabbath fast from the ninth day of the seventh month at sunset until the tenth day at sunset by specific command for just this one Sabbath (Leviticus 23:32).

We believe the communion is the Passover bread and wine—"Do this in remembrance of me." The Scripture that says, "As often as you do this," was written to people who knew only to partake of Unleavened Bread during the Passover season. This is the sign and seal of Yahweh on the forehead between the eyes and on the hand. Contrast this to those who keep it often and get the mark of the beast on the same places—forehead and hand (Exodus 13:9).

The Passover is on the fourteenth evening of the first month. The first month begins the first new moon after the green ears of barley have ripened as spring nears. There is no need to consider the equinox when the sun crosses the earth's equator. The first Hebrew month of every year takes place by nature, taking its course. Then one can look back and ask, "Did last year have twelve or thirteen months?" It is really that simple.

The annual Sabbaths then took their places as certain days of certain months, the first being the fifteenth and the second being the twenty-first of the first month. The next was Pentecost, the only one which is not a certain day of the third month but is counted fifty days after the weekly Sabbath falling between the fourteenth and the twenty-first of the first month. So, Pentecost always falls on a Sunday and results in two Sabbaths, one weekly and one annual, falling back-to-back. This is symbolic of the Jubilee when two years come together. Then the rest of the annual Sabbaths fell on certain days of the seventh month during the harvest.

The only annual Sabbath that did not begin at daybreak by specific command was the Sabbath rest and fast from the ninth evening to the tenth evening of the seventh month (Leviticus 23:32).

We believe there was a change in the Law out of necessity, just as there was a change in the priesthood (Hebrews 7:12).

The Laws that were changed were the sacrificial Laws regarding animals and birds. The Levitical priesthood is no more. It was replaced by Yahshua's sacrifice and finalized in 70 AD when the temple was destroyed and all priests were killed. From then on, Yahshua is the priest in the order of Melchizedek forever. He is the only priest until He anoints overcomers, kings, and priests for the millennium (the seventh one-thousand-year day).

We believe that any tithes must be paid to this Melchizedek priesthood and no other.

We believe that Peter was the first head of Yahshua's Church but that it is not Peter's church.

We believe that circumcision is still commanded for all eight-day-old males. The question presented to the early Church was, should an adult proselyte, especially Gentiles, be circumcised to be a member of the Church? Paul indicates circumcision was not required for adults, but it was never in question what the teaching was regarding newborns of any member of the Body of Christ. This pertains only to people who had already violated this Law by going past the eighth day.

Exodus 4:24 tells us that this is a matter of life and death to Yahweh, the God who is the same yesterday, today, and forever, when it says, "Yahweh was looking to murder Moses.

There is no prohibition against any adult male who wishes voluntarily to be circumcised.

We believe the dietary laws are still in effect, but breaking them is not a sin unto death. However not following these excellent health recommendations could lead to physical death. "The foods to be received with thanksgiving" (1 Timothy 4:3) means only clean foods are to be eaten with thanksgiving, not common or unclean foods. Peter, long after the resurrection, "never in his life ate anything common or unclean" (Acts 10:45). Only by realizing that his vision could not have anything to do with food could he realize that his vision only meant that the Gentiles should now be allowed into Christ's body of believers, something unthinkable to a Jew. The Bible explicitly tells us that this is what the vision meant.

We believe that the Father, the Son, and the Holy Spirit are three Gods in one Yahweh. This is not an explanation of how to understand the Trinity. It is just the correct way to say it. There is one Yahweh, not one God.

We believe that any churches that teach contrary to these beliefs are not Yahshua's Church.

When Yahshua returns, will He find the faith once delivered to His sheep (Luke 18:8)? Pray that you will hear His voice calling you. You have already taken step one by being born on planet Earth. Please take step two by being conceived again from above by the Holy Spirit. This is the only real purpose for us to come here.

We look forward to being changed in the twinkling of an eye at the last trump to be caught up in the air or wherever He goes from there to be with Yahshua our Lord and Savior forever.

ABOUT THE AUTHOR

Craig Swain was born on June 22, 1945, at the time when Germany and Japan surrendered during World War II. He was licensed to practice law on November 16, 1970. He is an undergraduate of Philosophy at a Catholic Monastery.

All of this schooling was intended to fulfill the requirements for a career in the FBI. However, his application was denied, resulting in a vacuum of goals. So he took a job as a trust officer for a couple of banks for five years and went about trying to solve the mysteries of the universe as a hobby.

After five years of working as a trust officer, Swain opened his own law office, and the real progress in his hobby took hold in 1978 when he heard the entire King James Bible *out loud*. Let this be a word to the wise.

The Clone is only a peripheral outcome, as Swain's real work is his book, *Then Is Finished the Mystery of God*, which under takes to understand the Bible as a whole with great emphasis on reconciling the issue of grace and law (law and grace), which are not opposite.

www.ingramcontent.com/pod-product-compliance
Lightning Source LLC
Chambersburg PA
CBHW051218120626
46547CB00013B/1408